CLASSICAL MYTHOLOGY

THE MYTHOLOGY LIBRARY
CLASSICAL
MYTHOLOGY

THE ANCIENT MYTHS AND LEGENDS OF GREECE AND ROME

ARTHUR COTTERELL

HERMES
HOUSE

This edition published by
Hermes House, an imprint
of Anness Publishing Limited
Hermes House, 88–89 Blackfriars
Road, London SE1 8HA

Published in the USA by
Hermes House, Anness
Publishing Inc.
27 West 20th Street,
New York, NY 10011

Publisher: Joanna Lorenz
Editorial Manager: Helen Sudell
Project Editor: Belinda Wilkinson
Designer: Nigel Soper, Millions Design
Illustrators: James Alexander,
Nick Beale, Glenn Steward

Previously published as part of
a larger compendium, *The
Encyclopedia of Mythology*

10 9 8 7 6 5 4 3 2 1

Page One: The Rape of Deianira
by Guido Reni
Frontispiece: Daedulas and Icarus
by Charles Landon
This page: The Rape of Ganymede
by Peter Paul Reubens

Author's Note
The entries in this encyclopedia are all
listed alphabetically. Where more than one
name exists for a character the entry is
listed under that used in the oringal
country of origin for that particular myth.
Names in italic capital letters indicate that
the name has an individual entry. Special
feature spreads examine specific
mythological themes in more detail. If a
character is included in a special feature
spread it is noted at the end of their
individual entry.

CONTENTS

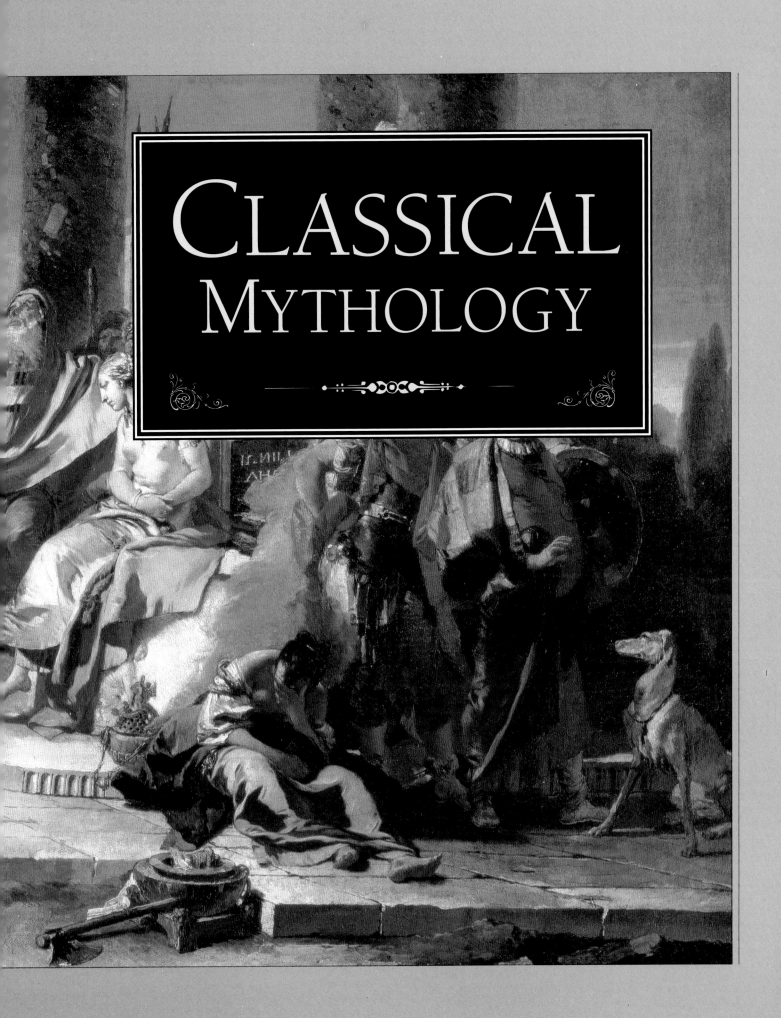

CLASSICAL
MYTHOLOGY

INTRODUCTION

THE ANCIENT GREEKS WERE THE great myth-makers of Europe. They even gave us the name by which we refer today to the amazing stories told about gods, heroes, men and animals. Around 400 BC the Athenian philosopher Plato coined the word *mythologia* in order to distinguish between imaginative accounts of divine actions and factual descriptions of events, supernatural or otherwise. Although he lived in an age that was increasingly scientific in outlook, and no longer inclined to believe every detail related about gods and goddesses, Plato recognized the power that resided in myth, and warned his followers to beware of its seductive charm.

The strength of Greek mythology, like all active traditions, lay in its collective nature. Unlike a story composed by a particular author, a myth always stood on its own, with a plot and a set of characters readily under-

MARS AND NEPTUNE, two gods of ancient Rome, ride over the Eternal City, guarding its military and maritime interests. At left, an airborne putto above Mars bears his horse's helmet, while Neptune's putto carries a seashell, symbol of the god's dominion over the waves. (MARS AND NEPTUNE BY PAOLO VERONESE, CANV.

ANCIENT GREECE

stood by those who listened to the story-teller or dramatist making use of it. When, for instance, the Athenians watched the great cycle of plays that Aeschylus staged about the murder of Agamemnon, they were already aware of the main characters and their actions. The audience knew how the House of Atreus, Agamemnon's father, was fated to endure a terrible period of domestic strife. Not only had Atreus and his brother Thyestes been cursed by their own father, Pelops, for killing his favourite child, their half-brother Chrysippus, but a bloody quarrel of their own had also added to the family misfortune. A dispute over the succession to Pelops' throne at Mycenae led Atreus to kill three of Thyestes' sons, although they had sought sanctuary in a temple dedicated to Zeus, the supreme god. Even worse, the murderer then served the bodies of his nephews up to his brother at a banquet, after which he dared to show Thyestes their feet and hands. Atreus paid for the outrage with his life at the hands of Thyestes' surviving son, Aegisthus, who later became the lover of Agamemnon's

wife Clytemnestra during his absence at the Trojan War.

All this would have been familiar to the Athenians before Aeschylus' treatment of the myth began with Agamemnon returning home from the Trojan War. Some of the audience doubtless recalled an even older curse laid on Pelops himself by the messenger god Hermes. Pelops had provoked the god by refusing a promised gift to one of his sons. Nothing that Aeschylus included in his plays was unexpected: neither the murder of Agamemnon, nor the revenge of his son Orestes, nor Orestes' pursuit by the Furies for shedding a mother's blood. What would have fascinated the audience was the dramatist's approach to these tangled incidents, his view of motive, guilt and expiation. For that reason another dramatist was able to tackle the same story later in Athens during the fifth century BC. It needs to be remembered that such drama remained very much part of ancient religion. Today we cannot expect to appreciate the full meaning of these performances, but we are fortunate in having the raw materials from which they were made, the myths themselves.

Myths retain much of their power, even when told in summary, as they are in this encyclopedia. Because Greek myths were fashioned and refashioned over so many generations, they acquired their essential form, a shape that had been collectively recognized for longer than anyone could remember. Even now, we continue to be fascinated by the stories of Oedipus, the man who murdered his father and married his mother; of the Athenian hero Theseus, slayer of the strange bull-headed man, the Minotaur; of the great voyager Jason, who sailed across the Black Sea to distant Colchis in order to fetch the Golden Fleece; of Agamemnon, the doomed leader of the Greek expedition against Troy; of cunning Odysseus, one of the bravest of the Greeks and the inventor of the Wooden Horse, the means by which Troy was taken; of the hapless Pentheus, victim of Dionysus' ecstatic worshippers, who included his own mother; of the unbeatable champion Achilles; of the labours of Heracles, Zeus' own son and the only hero to be granted immortality; and many others. As Greeks living before and after Plato evidently understood, myths were fictitious stories that illustrated truth.

The Romans were no less impressed by the range and interest of Greek mythology. Indeed, they adopted it wholesale and identified many of their own Italian deities with those in the Greek pantheon, even adopting others for whom they possessed no real equivalent. The unruly Dionysus gave Rome considerable trouble. This god of vegetation, wine and ecstasy was by no means a comfortable deity for the Greeks, but the Romans were more deeply disturbed by his orgiastic rites. In 186 BC the Roman Senate passed severe laws against the excesses of his worshippers. It is likely that several thousand

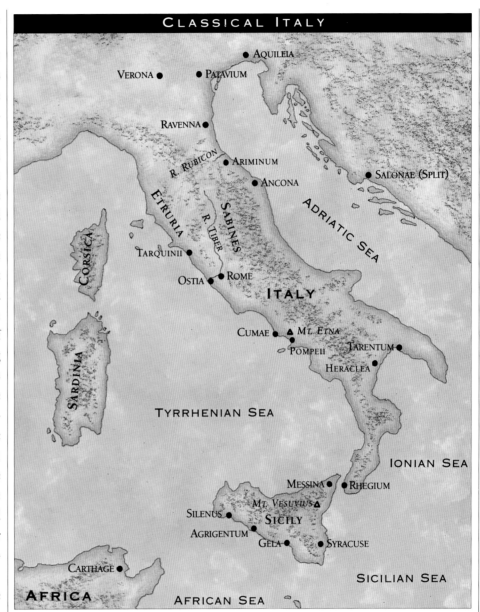

CLASSICAL ITALY

people were executed before the cult of the native wine god Bacchus discarded those aspects of Dionysus which met with official disproval. This taming of a Greek god, albeit Thracian in origin, could stand for the entire process by which Greek and Roman mythology merged in the second century BC. There were just too many myths for the Romans to resist, although they chose to impose a typical restraint on Greek extravagance.

Roman heroes could never compare with Heracles, Jason, Theseus, Perseus or Bellerophon. Something synthetic can be felt in the story of Aeneas, the leader of the refugees from Troy. His adoption as a founder-hero made him of particular concern to the first Roman emperor Augustus, but *The Aeneid*, the epic poem about Aeneas written by Virgil in the 20s BC, turned out to be a balanced celebration of Roman authority rather than an exciting heroic narrative. The hero heeded the call of duty and abandoned the woman he loved, as Roman heroes were expected to do in every myth.

A

ACHILLES was the son of King Peleus of Thessaly and the sea nymph *THETIS*. He was the greatest of the Greek warriors, although in comparison with *AGAMEMNON* and the other Greek kings who went on the expedition against Troy, he appears to have been something of a barbarian. His anger was as legendary as his prowess.

The uncertain nature of Achilles is apparent in the story of his birth. Both *ZEUS* and *POSEIDON* wanted to have a son by the beautiful Thetis, but *PROMETHEUS*, the fire god, had warned them that her offspring would be greater than his father. Anxious to avoid the emergence of a power superior to themselves, the gods carefully arranged the marriage of Thetis to a mortal. Because she was so attached to Achilles, Thetis tried to make him immortal by various means. The best known was dipping the new-born baby in the Styx, the river that ran through *HADES*, the world of the dead. Since Thetis had to hold him by the heel, this one spot was left vulnerable and at Troy brought about Achilles' death from a poisoned arrow shot from the bow of *PARIS*.

Achilles learned the skills of warfare from *CHIRON*, leader of the *CENTAURS*, who also fed him on wild game to increase his ferocity. Under Chiron's care Achilles became renowned as a courageous fighter, but his immortal mother knew that he was doomed to die at Troy if he went on the expedition. So Thetis arranged for him to be disguised as a girl and hidden among the women at the palace of King Lycomedes on the island of Scyros. The Greeks felt that without Achilles their chances of beating the Trojans were slim, but no one could identify the hidden hero. At last, cunning *ODYSSEUS* was sent to discover Achilles, which he did by means of a trick.

Having traced the young man to Scyros, Odysseus placed weapons among some jewellery in the palace. While Achilles' female companions were admiring the craftsmanship of the jewels, a call to arms was sounded and the warrior quickly reached for the weapons, giving himself away. Unmasked, Achilles had no choice but to sail for Troy.

There he bitterly quarrelled with Agamemnon, the leader of the Greeks. It may be that he was angered by Agamemnon's use of his name to bring *IPHIGENIA* to Aulis, for she had been told she was to marry Achilles, whereas Agamemnon intended to sacrifice

ACHILLES, relaxing beside his tent with his companion, Patroclus, welcomes his comrades, Odysseus (centre) and Ajax (right), who implore the moody hero to return to battle where he is sorely needed.
(ACHILLES RECEIVES AGAMEMNON'S MESSENGERS, BY JEAN-AUGUST INGRES, CANVAS, 1801.)

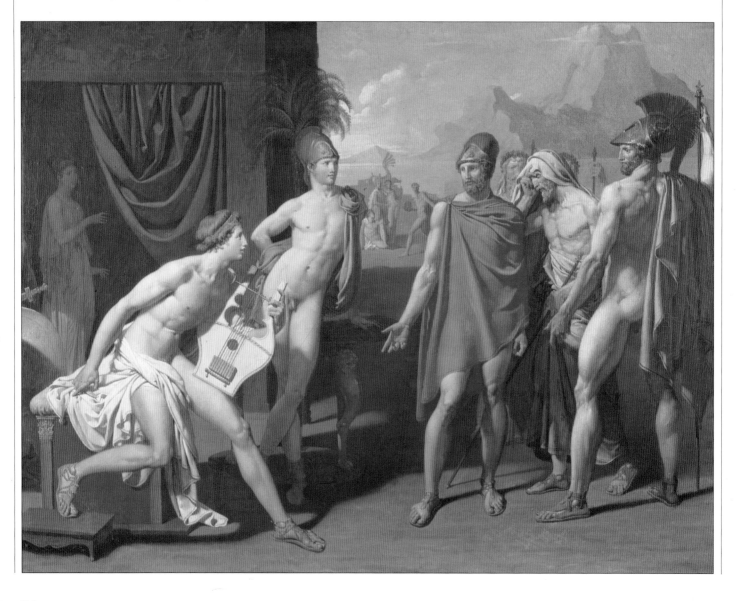

her to the goddess *ARTEMIS*, to ensure a favourable wind for the Greek fleet. For a long time Achilles stayed in his tent and refused to fight the Trojans. He even persuaded his mother to use her influence with Zeus to let the tide of war go against the Greeks. But Achilles was roused to action by the death of Patroclus, his squire and lover, at the hands of the Trojan *HECTOR*. Patroclus had borrowed Achilles' armour, which had been forged by the smith god *HEPHAISTOS*, and entered the fray, but he came up against Hector who easily defeated him.

In brand-new armour Achilles sought out Hector, who asked for respect to be shown for his body if he was defeated. Achilles refused, slew Hector with his spear and dragged the Trojan hero round the tomb of Patroclus for twelve days. Only Thetis could persuade her son to let the Trojans recover the corpse and arrange a funeral, a serious obligation for the living.

Back in the fight, Achilles struck fear into the Trojans, of whom he killed hundreds. But his own life was coming to an end, which he

ACHILLES falls beneath the Trojan walls, shot by Paris. The sun god aims his arrow straight for Achilles' heel, the only mortal part of the hero's body. In some myths, Apollo guided Paris' bow; in others, the god shot the arrow, as seen here. (APOLLO SLAYS ACHILLES BY FRANZ STASSEN, WATERCOLOUR, 1869.)

ACTAEON was a young Greek hunter who unluckily chanced upon the pool where Artemis and her nymphs were bathing. In outrage, the virgin goddess turned him into a stag and he was torn apart by his own hounds. (ILLUSTRATION FROM DICTIONARY OF CLASSICAL ANTIQUITIES, 1891.)

had been warned about by his steed *XANTHUS*, before the *FURIES* struck the divine creature dumb. An arrow from the bow of Paris, guided by the god of prophecy *APOLLO*, gave Achilles a mortal wound. Heroic yet also arrogant, Achilles was the mythical figure most admired by Alexander the Great. At the commencement of his Asian campaign against the Persians, the youthful Alexander participated in funeral games that were held at Troy in memory of Achilles. (See also *HEROES*)

ACTAEON

ACTAEON was the son of a minor royal god and Autonoe, daughter of *CADMUS*. A Greek hunter trained by *CHIRON*, he offended the goddess *ARTEMIS* and paid with his life. There are several reasons given for his terrible end. Actaeon may have boasted of his superior skill as a hunter, or annoyed the goddess by seeing her bathing naked. To stop his boasting, Artemis turned him into a stag and he was chased and devoured by his own hounds. But these faithful animals were broken-hearted at the loss of their master, until Chiron carved a statue of Actaeon so lifelike that they were satisfied.

AEGEUS

AEGEUS was the son of King Pandion of Athens, and father of the hero *THESEUS*. Having twice married without begetting any children, Aegeus went to consult the Delphic Oracle but received only the ambiguous answer that he should not untie his wine skin until he reached home. When he sought advice from his friend Pittheus, another ruler, the latter realized that the oracle had foretold how Aegeus would father a heroic son. To secure the services of such a man, Pittheus made Aegeus drunk and let him sleep with his daughter Aethra. When Aegeus understood what had happened, he placed a sword and a pair of sandals beneath an enormous boulder. He told the princess that if she bore a son who could move the rock, he was to bring these tokens to him in Athens on reaching manhood. Thus it was that Theseus grew up and was eventually reunited with his father.

Meantime, Aegeus had married the sorceress *MEDEA*, whose magical powers had given him another son, Medus. It was for this reason that Medea did everything she could to thwart Theseus. At her

suggestion Theseus was sent to fight the wild bull of Marathon, which he captured alive. Once Aegeus recognized his son, Medea returned in disgust to her native Colchis on the Black Sea. But bad luck continued to dog Aegeus and eventually caused his death. For it was agreed that Theseus should travel to Crete with the seven girls and seven boys sent as tribute each year to feed the *MINOTAUR*, a bull-headed man. If Theseus was successful in his dangerous mission to kill the Minotaur, the ship bringing him home was to fly a white sail; if unsuccessful, a black sail would signal his death. Returning to Athens after an incredible adventure in the Labyrinth at Knossos, Theseus forgot the agreement to change his sail from black to white, with the result that, upon seeing the vessel with its black sail, Aegeus threw himself off the Athenian acropolis to certain death.

AEGEUS, looking out to sea, sees his son's ships returning home, all with black sails hoisted. Thinking that his son had died, Aegeus hurled himself into the sea, afterwards named the Aegean. (ILLUSTRATION BY NICK BEALE, 1995.)

AENEAS gazes in wonder at the decorative temple in Carthage, while Dido, the queen, welcomes him to her exotic kingdom. Around them, pillars, doors and beams are made of bronze, while the fabulous walls are decorated with the famous tale of Aeneas and the Trojans.

(ILLUSTRATION BY NICK BEALE, 1995.)

AENEAS was a Trojan hero and the son of Anchises and *VENUS*, the Roman goddess of love. He was the favourite of the Romans, who believed that some of their eminent families were descended from the Trojans who fled westwards with him from Asia Minor, after the Greek sack of their city. Upstart Rome was only too aware of its lack of tradition and history in comparison with Greece (there was a notable absence of a glorious past peopled with mythical heroes and gods), so the exploits of Aeneas conveniently provided a means of reasserting national pride. It was not a coincidence that the first Roman emperor, Augustus, took a personal interest in the myth.

During the Trojan War Anchises was unable to fight, having been rendered blind or lame for boasting about his relationship with Venus. But young Aeneas distinguished himself against the Greeks, who feared him second only to *HECTOR*, the Trojan champion. In gratitude *PRIAM* gave Aeneas his daughter Creusa to have as his wife, and a son was born named *ASCANIUS*. Although Venus warned him of the impending fall of Troy, Anchises refused to quit the city until two omens occurred: a small flame rose from the top of Ascanius' head and a meteor fell close by. So, carrying Anchises on his back, Aeneas managed to escape Troy with his father and his son. Somehow Creusa became separated from the party and disappeared. Later, Aeneas saw her ghost and learned from it that he would found a new Troy in distant Italy.

After sailing through the Aegean Sea, where the small fleet Aeneas commanded stopped at a number of islands, the fleet came to Epirus on the eastern Adriatic coast. From there it made for Sicily, but before reaching the Italian mainland it was diverted to North Africa during a sudden storm sent by the goddess *JUNO*, the Roman equivalent of *HERA*, who harassed Aeneas throughout the voyage. Only the timely help of *NEPTUNE*, the Roman sea god, saved the fleet from shipwreck. At the city of Carthage, the great trading port founded by the Phoenicians (which was located in present-day Tunisia), Venus ensured that Aeneas fell in love with its beautiful queen, the widow *DIDO*. Because of her own flight to Carthage, Dido welcomed the Trojan refugees with great kindness and unlimited hospitality.

Time passed pleasantly for the lovers, as Aeneas and Dido soon became, and it seemed as if Italy and the new state to be founded on its shores were both forgotten. But watchful *JUPITER*, the chief Roman god, dispatched *MERCURY* with a message to Aeneas, recalling him to his duty and commanding him to resume the voyage. Horrified by his intention to leave, Dido bitterly reproached Aeneas, but his deep sense of piety gave him strength enough to launch the fleet again. Then the weeping queen mounted a pyre which she had ordered to be prepared and, having run herself through with a sword, was consumed by the flames.

When the Trojans finally landed in Italy, near the city of Cumae, Aeneas went to consult the *SIBYL*, who was a renowned prophetess. She took him on a visit to the

AENEAS and his comrades battle with a flock of raging harpies who hover above them in the sky, waiting to carry off the weak and wounded. Beside Aeneas shelter his family: his blind father Anchises, his wife Creusa and their two sons. (AENEAS AND HIS COMPANIONS FIGHT THE HARPIES BY FRANCOIS PERRIER, CANVAS, 1646-47.)

AGAMEMNON watches coolly as his daughter, Iphigenia, is offered as a "sacrificial lamb" to appease the anger of Artemis; but at the last moment, the goddess herself relented and, descending from heaven, she carried Iphigenia off to Taurus. (THE SACRIFICE OF IPHIGENIA BY GIOVANNI BATTISTA, TEMPERA, 1770.)

underworld. There Aeneas met his father's ghost, who showed him the destiny of Rome. Anchises had died of old age during the stay in Sicily, but his enthusiastic outline of the future encouraged his son. Aeneas also saw Dido's ghost, but it did not speak to him and hurriedly turned away.

Afterwards, Aeneas steered for the mouth of the River Tiber, on whose river banks the city of Rome would be built centuries later. Conflict with the Latins, the local inhabitants, was bloody and prolonged. But peace was made when Aeneas married Lavinia, the daughter of King Latinus. It had been foretold that for the sake of the kingdom Lavinia must marry a man from abroad. The Trojans, in order to appease Juno, adopted the Latins' traditions and language. (See also *VOYAGERS*)

AGAMEMNON, according to Greek mythology, was the son of *ATREUS* and the brother of *MENELAUS*, king of Sparta. He was married to *CLYTEMNESTRA*. From his citadel at Mycenae, or nearby Argos, he sent out a summons to the Greeks to join the expedition against Troy. The cause of the war was the flight of Menelaus' wife, *HELEN*, to that city with *PARIS*.

However, the Greek fleet was delayed at Aulis by contrary winds. Agamemnon then realized that he would have to make a human sacrifice in order to appease *ARTEMIS*, the goddess of the forest and wild animals. His daughter *IPHIGENIA* was therefore sent to Aulis under the pretext that she was to be married to the Greek champion and hero *ACHILLES*. According to one tradition, Iphigenia was sacrificed, but according to another, she was saved by Artemis herself and taken to Taurus to become a priestess in the goddess's temple.

Clytemnestra never forgave Agamemnon for Iphigenia's loss, and she took Aegisthus for a lover during the ten-year siege of Troy. Aegisthus was the son of Thyestes, the brother and enemy of Atreus,

Agamemnon's father. On her husband's return, Clytemnestra at first pretended how pleased she was to see him. Thanking the gods for his safe return, Agamemnon crossed the threshold of his palace, ignoring the warning of his slave *CASSANDRA*, the prophetic daughter of *PRIAM*, the defeated Trojan king. He then retired to a bathroom in order to change his clothes. Clytemnestra quickly threw a large net over Agamemnon and twisted

AJAX heads off the Trojan onslaught with typical might and courage. Beside him, his brother, Teucer the archer, aims his bow at the Trojans who, with flaming torches, hope to set the Greek ships alight. (ILLUSTRATION FROM STORIES FROM HOMER, 1885.)

it around his body, rendering him an easy target for Aegisthus' axe.

AJAX was the son of Telamon of Salamis and, like *ACHILLES*, was a powerful aid to the Greeks in their assault on Troy. After Achilles' death there was a contest for the armour of this great warrior, which had been forged by the smith god *HEPHAISTOS*. When *ODYSSEUS* was awarded the armour, Ajax became mad with jealousy. He planned a night attack on his comrades, but the goddess *ATHENA* deceived him into slaughtering a flock of sheep instead. In the light of dawn, Ajax was suddenly overwhelmed by a fear of his evil intentions, and fell on his sword and died.

ALCESTIS, according to Greek mythology, was the daughter of King Pelias of Thessaly. When she was of an age to marry, many suitors appeared and her father set a test to discover who would be the most suitable husband. Alcestis was to be the wife of the first man to yoke a lion and a boar (or, in some versions, a bear) to a chariot. With the aid of *APOLLO*, the god of prophecy, a neighbouring monarch named Admetus succeeded in this seemingly impossible task. But at the wedding he forgot to make the necessary sacrifice in gratitude to *ARTEMIS*, the goddess of the forest and wild animals, and so found his wedding bed full of snakes. Once again Apollo came to the king's assistance and, by making the *FATES* drunk, extracted from them a promise that if anyone else would die on Admetus' behalf, he might continue to live. As no one would volunteer, Alcestis gave her life for him. *PERSEPHONE*, the underworld goddess, was so impressed by this complete devotion that she restored Alcestis to Admetus, and they had two sons who later took part in the Greek expedition against the city of Troy.

ALCESTIS (below) welcomes her suitor, Admetus, who arrives in a chariot drawn by lions and bears, while Alcestis' father, Pelias, looks on in disbelief. Admetus was the only hero to yoke the beasts, so winning the hand of Alcestis. (ILLUSTRATION FROM STORIES FROM GREECE AND ROME, 1920.)

ALCMENE was the daughter of Electryon, son of *PERSEUS*, and the mother of *HERACLES*. She married Amphitryon, king of Tiryns, near Mycenae in the Peloponnese. Alcmene refused to consummate her marriage to Amphitryon until he had avenged the murder of her brothers. This the king did, but when he returned he was amazed to learn from Alcmene that she believed she had already slept with him. Amphitryon was enraged until the seer *TIRESIAS* explained that *ZEUS* had come to Alcmene disguised as her husband in order to father a mortal who would aid the gods in their forthcoming battle against the *GIANTS*.

So Alcmene became pregnant with twins: Heracles, the son of Zeus, and Iphicles, the son of Amphitryon. Zeus could not hide his satisfaction from his wife *HERA* who realized what had happened. She sent the goddess of childbirth, Eileithyia, to frustrate the delivery, but a trick saved Alcmene and her two sons. Hera then put snakes into Heracles' cradle, but the infant hero strangled them.

Zeus never let Hera fatally injure Heracles, and always protected Alcmene. Once Amphitryon tried to burn her for infidelity, but was stopped by a sudden downpour. When Alcmene died naturally of old age, Zeus sent *HERMES* to bring her body to the Elysian Fields.

ALCMENE (right) was one of the sky god Zeus' many lovers, but was punished for her infidelity by her angry husband, Amphitryon, who here is portrayed setting alight a pyre beneath her. She was saved by a heavenly downpour sent by Zeus. (ILLUSTRATION BY NICK BEALE, 1995.)

THE AMAZONS (opposite), fierce and independent maiden warriors, fought with passion and skill. In early images, they appear in exotic Scythian leotards, bearing half-moon shields, but in later Greek art, they wore Dorian chitons, with one shoulder bare, as seen here. (THE BATTLE OF THE AMAZONS BY PETER PAUL RUBENS, WOOD, 1600.)

AMULIUS (left) casts out his nephews, Romulus and Remus, the twin sons of Rhea Silvia and the war god Mars, ordering that they be drowned in the river Tiber. But they are eventually found by a she-wolf who suckles them until a shepherd, Faustulus, takes them home. (ILLUSTRATION FROM STORIES FROM LIVY, 1885.)

THE AMAZONS were a tribe of female warriors, supposedly descended from *ARES*, the Greek war god, and the *NAIAD* Harmonia. Their home was situated beyond the Black Sea. It is thought that their name refers to their breastless condition, for Amazons voluntarily removed their right breasts in order that they might more easily draw a bow. The ancient Greeks believed these fierce warriors periodically mated with the men from another tribe, afterwards rearing their female children but discarding or maiming all the males.

During the Trojan War they fought against the Greeks. Although he killed the Amazon queen Penthesilea, *ACHILLES* never succeeded in shaking off the rumour that he had been in love with her. He even slew a comrade who mentioned it. Fascination with Amazon power affected other heroes besides Achilles. The adventures of both *HERACLES* and *THESEUS* involved battles with Amazons. One of Heracles' famous labours was the seizure of a girdle belonging to the Amazon queen Hippolyta, a theft that required considerable nerve.

AMULIUS, in Roman mythology, was a descendant of the Trojan hero *AENEAS*. He usurped the throne of Alba Longa from his younger brother Numitor and forced Numitor's daughter *RHEA SILVIA* to become a Vestal Virgin so as to deny her father an heir. When Rhea Silvia was raped by the war god *MARS*, Amulius imprisoned her and ordered that her twin sons, *REMUS AND ROMULUS*, be drowned in the Tiber. But the two boys escaped a watery death and grew up in the countryside. Once they realized their parentage, Romulus and Remus returned to Alba Longa and killed their uncle Amulius.

ANDROMACHE, the daughter of Eetion, a king of Mysia in Asia Minor, was the wife of *HECTOR*, the foremost Trojan warrior. Her entire family – parents, brothers, husband and son – was killed during the Trojan War. After the sack of Troy, Andromache was taken off into captivity by Neoptolemus, the son of the great Greek hero *ACHILLES*. Neoptolemus had shown the same violent and tempestuous temper as his father when he ruthlessly killed the Trojan king, *PRIAM*, at the altar of *ZEUS*' temple. Andromache bore Neoptolemus three sons, and in consequence suffered the hatred of his barren Greek wife. When Neoptolemus died, Andromache went on to marry Helenus who, like her, was a Trojan captive. Her final years were spent in Asia Minor at Pergamum, which was a new city founded by one of her sons.

ANDROMACHE, Hector's young wife, bows her head in captivity. One of the noblest but most ill-starred of heroines, she sees her husband, father and seven brothers killed by Achilles, and her son hurled from the city walls; while she falls as a prize of war to Achilles' son. (CAPTIVE ANDROMACHE BY LORD LEIGHTON, CANVAS, C. 1890.)

ANTIGONE (above) sprinkles earth on the body of her brother, Polynices, as a symbolic act of burial. For the Greeks, burial was a sacred duty, without which a soul could not rest; yet Creon, her uncle, had denied Polynices a burial, violating divine law. (ILLUSTRATION BY NICK BEALE, 1995.)

ANDROMEDA (left), chained to a rock as a sacrifice to a sea monster,' can only pray, while high overhead, the hero Perseus is on his way. Swooping down on the winged horse, Pegasus, he cuts Andromeda free and slays the monster. (PERSEUS RELEASES ANDROMEDA BY JOACHIM WIEWAEL, CANVAS, 1630.)

in an uprising against the new ruler CREON, and his body was condemned to rot unburied outside the city. Antigone refused to accept this impiety and sprinkled earth over the corpse as a token burial. For this she was walled up in a cave, where she hanged herself like her mother Jocasta. There are a number of different versions of the myth, but they all cast Antigone as the heroic victim of a family wrecked by a terrible deed.

ANTIOPE see LOVERS OF ZEUS

APHRODITE was the Greek goddess of love, beauty and fertility. Unlike her Roman counterpart VENUS, with whom she was identified, Aphrodite was not only a goddess of sexual love but also of the affection that sustains social life. The meaning of her name is uncertain, although the ancient Greeks came to believe it referred to foam. Quite possibly this belief arose from the story of Aphrodite's

ANDROMEDA was the daughter of Cassiope and Cepheus, king of the Ethiopians. When Cassiope boasted that Andromeda was more beautiful than the Nereids, the sea nymphs, they complained to the sea god POSEIDON. He avenged this insult by flooding the land and sending a sea monster to devastate Cepheus' kingdom. To avoid complete disaster it was decided to sacrifice Andromeda to the beast and she was chained to a rock at the foot of a cliff. There PERSEUS saw her as he flew past on winged sandals carrying the head of the Gorgon Medusa. He fell in love with Andromeda, and obtained both her and her father's consent to marriage if he defeated the monster. This Perseus did by using Medusa's head, the sight of which turned all living things to stone. After some time, Perseus and Andromeda settled in Tiryns, which Perseus ruled. The constellation of Andromeda lies close to that of Pegasus, and both Cepheus and Cassiope were also commemorated in the stars.

ANTIGONE was the daughter of OEDIPUS, king of Thebes, and his wife and mother Jocasta. On learning of their unwitting incest, Oedipus tore out his eyes while Jocasta hanged herself. The penitent Oedipus was then guided by Antigone in his wanderings round Greece. She was with him at the sanctuary of Colonus, near Athens, when her distraught father gained some kind of peace just before his death. She returned to Thebes, but her troubles were not over. Her brother Polynices had been killed

APHRODITE, goddess of love and beauty, was born from the foam of the sea; she rose from the waves on a seashell, stepping ashore on Cyprus. At her side, the west wind, Zephyrus, and Flora, the spring, blow her gently ashore in a shower of roses, her sacred flower. (THE BIRTH OF VENUS BY SANDRO BOTTICELLI, TEMPERA, C. 1482.)

birth. When the Titan *CRONOS* cut off the penis of his father Ouranos with a sharp sickle, he cast the immortal member into the sea, where it floated amid white foam. Inside the penis Aphrodite grew and was then washed up at Paphos on Cyprus. There were in fact sanctuaries dedicated to her on many islands, which suggests that she was a West Asian goddess who was brought to Greece by sea-traders.

Once she arrived, the ancient Greeks married her in their mythology to the crippled smith god *HEPHAISTOS*. But Aphrodite was not content to be a faithful wife and she bore children by several other gods, including *DIONYSUS* and *ARES*. When Hephaistos found out about Aphrodite's passion for the war god Ares, the outraged smith god made a mesh of gold and caught the lovers in bed together. He called the other gods from Mount Olympus to see the pair, but they only laughed at his shame, and *POSEIDON*, the god of the sea, persuaded Hephaistos to release Aphrodite and Ares.

Perhaps Aphrodite's greatest love was for the handsome youth Adonis, another West Asian deity. Killed by a wild boar, Adonis became the object of admiration for both Aphrodite and *PERSEPHONE*, queen of the dead. Their bitter quarrel was only ended by *ZEUS*, who ruled that for a third of the year Adonis was to dwell with himself, for a third part with Persephone, and for a third part with Aphrodite. So it was that the ancient Greeks accommodated a West Asian mother goddess and her dying-and-rising husband. Indeed the Adonia, or annual festivals commemorating Adonis' death, were celebrated in many parts of the eastern Mediterranean.

Because of her unruly behaviour, Zeus caused Aphrodite to fall in love with Anchises, the father of *AENEAS*. In the Roman version of this myth Venus herself is deeply attracted to the Trojan, but warns him to keep the parentage of their son Aeneas a secret. This Anchises fails to do, and as a result suffers blindness or a disability of the limbs. While the Roman goddess provided, through the leadership of Aeneas, a means for some of the Trojans to escape and flourish anew in Italy, the Greek Aphrodite actually helped to cause the Trojan War. In order to ensure that he would name her as the most beautiful of the goddesses, Aphrodite promised *PARIS*, son of *PRIAM* the king of Troy, the hand of the most beautiful woman in the world. This fatefully turned out to be *HELEN*, wife of *MENELAUS*, king of Sparta.

APOLLO

APOLLO was the son of *ZEUS* and the Titaness *LETO*, and the twin brother of the goddess *ARTEMIS*, the virgin huntress. He was one of the most important deities of both the Greek and Roman religions, and was the god of prophecy, archery and music. The origin of his name is uncertain but it is probably non-European.

A fight with the gigantic earth-serpent Python at Delphi gave Apollo the seat of his famous oracle. Python was an offspring of *GAIA*, mother earth, which issued revelations through a fissure in the rock so that a priestess, the Pythia, could give answers to any questions that might be asked. After he slew the earth-serpent, Apollo took its place, though he had to do penance in Thessaly for the killing. Indeed, Zeus twice forced Apollo to be the slave of a mortal man to pay for his crime.

Apollo's interest in healing suggests an ancient association with the plague and its control. His son *ASCLEPIUS* was also identified with healing and connected with sites in northern Greece. Indeed, so accomplished was Asclepius in medicine that Zeus slew him with a thunderbolt for daring to bring a man back to life. (See also *FORCES OF NATURE*)

ARES

ARES, the son of *ZEUS* and *HERA*, was the Greek god of war, and was later identified with the Roman war god *MARS*. Although Ares had no wife of his own, he had three children by *APHRODITE*, the goddess of love. The twins, Phobos, "panic", and Deimos, "fear", always accompanied him on the battlefield. In Greek mythology, Ares is depicted as an instigator of violence, a tempestuous and passionate lover and an unscrupulous friend. The Roman god Mars, however, has nothing of Ares' fickleness.

APOLLO (above), the sun god, urges the sun-chariot to rise in the sky. This unusual version of the myth has Apollo, rather than Helios, as rider, and lions, instead of horses, pull the chariot, recalling the link between Leo and the sun. (PHOEBUS APOLLO BY BRITON RIVIERE, CANVAS, C. 1870.)

ARES (below), in full armour, leads the gods into battle. However, in war, the gods were not impartial; Ares, Aphrodite (left), Poseidon and Apollo (centre) would often aid the Trojans, while Hera and Athena (right) supported the Greeks. (ILLUSTRATION FROM STORIES FROM HOMER, 1885.)

LOVERS OF ZEUS

A STRIKING ASPECT OF GREEK MYTHOLOGY is the marital conflict between the two chief deities, Hera, an earth goddess, and her husband, Zeus, supreme power on Olympus. One of the most amorous gods in mythology, Zeus loved countless women and he courted them in as many forms, sometimes as a bull, as a satyr, as a swan, sometimes as a mortal man, and even in the form of a golden shower. Hera was notoriously jealous and vengeful, pursuing without mercy his lovers and their offspring. The antagonism between the two could be viewed as a clash between different religious traditions or local cults, each cult recognizing a different lover who was often regarded as the ancestor of a ruling family.

ANTIOPE (above), *daughter of a river god, was loved by Zeus in the form of a satyr, a goat-like creature. She bore him twin sons, Amphion and Zethus. Here, Zeus, disguised as a youthful satyr, gently shades Antiope from the sun while she sleeps beside Eros, sweet god of love.* (ANTIOPE SHADED BY ZEUS DISGUISED AS A SATYR BY ANTONIO CORREGGIO, CANVAS, 1523-25.)

CALLISTO (above), *forest nymph and companion of Artemis in the chase, was loved by Zeus and bore him a son, Arcas. She was then changed into a bear either by Zeus, wishing to hide her from Hera, or by Hera herself. As a bear she was shot by Artemis in the forest and was placed among the stars as the She-Bear. Here, surrounded by the trophies of the chase, Artemis and her nymphs comfort Callisto possibly after her encounter with the overwhelming god, Zeus.* (DIANA AND CALLISTO BY PETER PAUL RUBENS, CANVAS, 1636-40.)

EUROPA (right) *was wooed by Zeus in the shape of a beautiful bull who emerged from the waves and carried her over the sea to Crete where she bore him three sons. The various stages of the drama are represented here: on the left, Europa mounts the bull encouraged by its tameness. On the right, she is borne sedately down to the sea, with many little Erotes (love spirits) hovering in the sky. Finally she floats happily away, waving to her maidens.* (THE RAPE OF EUROPA BY PAOLO VERONESE, CANVAS, 1580.)

DIONYSUS (above), Zeus' child by Semele, appears here hugging his mother, while Apollo stands by with a bay tree. Once he became a god, Dionysus raised his mother to heaven and placed her among the stars as Thyone. This Etruscan mirror is bordered with ivy, which was Dionysus' sacred plant. (ILLUSTRATION FROM DR SMITH'S CLASSICAL DICTIONARY, 1895.)

DANAE (below) was confined in a brazen tower by her father who feared an oracle predicting that he would be killed by a grandson. In her tower she was visited by Zeus in the form of a golden shower, and bore him a son, Perseus. When her father discovered the baby, he cast both of them out to sea in a wooden chest, but they floated ashore on the Isle of Seriphos where they were rescued by Dictys. (ILLUSTRATION BY GEORGE SOPER FROM TANGLEWOOD TALES, C. 1920.)

SEMELE (left), encouraged by Hera, persuaded Zeus to show himself in all his splendour. When he appeared before her as the radiant god of thunder and lightning, Semele was consumed by the flames and, dying, gave birth prematurely to Dionysus, whom Zeus saved from the fire. In this powerful Symbolist version of the myth, the great god radiates fiery, blood-red lightning. A winged child hiding from the light could be Dionysus, while the dark, horned god seems to be a fusion of Hades and Pan. (JUPITER AND SEMELE, BY GUSTAVE MOREAU, CANVAS, 1896.)

THE ARGONAUTS were very early explorers, most likely the first Greek voyagers to the Black Sea. They sailed from Thessaly, where their leader, *JASON*, was the rightful king of Iolcus. According to the myth, Jason's father, Aeson, was deposed by his half-brother Pelias, who was warned at the time how he would in turn be overthrown by a man wearing only one sandal. In order to protect Jason from Pelias, Aeson had secretly sent his son to *CHIRON* to educate the young man, like many other heroes. On reaching manhood, Jason determined to return to Iolcus and reclaim the throne. During the journey, however, he was tested by the goddess *HERA*, who was disguised as an old woman. She begged him to carry her safely across a swollen river,

THE ARGONAUTS (top) commissioned Argus to build the Argo, a ship with twenty oars. Here he carves out the stern, while Athena makes sails. Behind her, perched on a pillar, her sacred creature, the owl, symbolizes her wisdom. (ILLUSTRATION FROM DICTIONARY OF CLASSICAL ANTIQUITIES, 1891.)

JASON (above left), helps Hera, disguised as an old woman, across the stream. In the current he loses a sandal, fulfilling part of an oracle that a half-shod man would take Pelias' throne. The peacock beside Hera denotes her all-seeing vision. (ILLUSTRATION FROM TANGLEWOOD TALES, C. 1920.)

JASON (above), with Medea's help – she anoints him with a salve to protect him from fire and steel – ploughs the fields with the bulls of Aietes. He was the first hero to yoke the wild and fiery creatures.
(ILLUSTRATION FROM TANGLEWOOD TALES, C. 1920.)

which Jason did at the cost of one of his sandals. Thus the prophecy was fulfilled: a man wearing only one sandal arrived at Iolcus to challenge Pelias. Because Jason made his intentions known at the time of a religious festival, Pelias could not kill his nephew without the risk of suffering divine disfavour. So the king told Jason that he could have the throne provided he obtained the Golden Fleece, which was an apparently impossible task. This miraculous fleece belonged to a ram which had flown to Colchis, a distant land identified with modern Georgia. It hung from a tree there, guarded by an enormous snake that never slept.

The *DELPHIC ORACLE* encouraged Jason to undertake the quest. Hera inspired a group of Thessalian

ARIADNE (above) hands the vital skein to Theseus, which allows him to track his way through the Labyrinth. After killing the bull-like beast, the Minotaur, in the Labyrinth, he sailed away with her, but then deserted her on Dia, possibly believing that she was destined to marry a god.
(ILLUSTRATION FROM TANGLEWOOD TALES, C. 1920.)

warriors to join his expedition and they became known as the Argonauts, the crew of the ship *Argo*. Among their number were Castor and Polydeuces, *ORPHEUS* the poet, Calais and Zetes the sons of *BOREAS* and the hero *HERACLES*. Together they crossed a sea of marvels, visited strange lands and overcame many obstacles before reaching Colchis, where Hera used the goddess of love *APHRODITE* to make *MEDEA*, the second daughter

of King Aietes, fall in love with Jason. The king hated Greeks but he kept his feelings hidden from the Argonauts. He even consented to Jason's attempt to capture the Golden Fleece. But first Aietes set Jason a challenge that was intended to result in his death. The hero was required to yoke a team of fire-breathing bulls, plough and sow a field with dragon's teeth, and slay the armed men who would at once rise from the ground.

With the assistance of Medea's skills in the magic arts, Jason accomplished Aietes' task within a single day. But the king of Colchis was not prepared to give up the Golden Fleece so easily. He secretly planned to attack the Argonauts, who were warned by Medea, now Jason's lover. She employed her magic once again to deal with the unsleeping snake, and Jason seized the Golden Fleece. The Argonauts quickly rowed away from Colchis with the fleece and Medea, whom Jason had promised to marry once back in Thessaly.

The Colchian princess seems to have been associated with the rites of dismemberment as well as magic, for during the pursuit of the Argonauts across the Black Sea, Medea slowed the fleet of her father Aietes by killing and cutting up her own brother, Apsyrtus. Pieces of Apsyrtus' body were thrown overboard, forcing the Colchians to gather up the remains for a decent burial. Later, in Thessaly, Medea also persuaded the daughters of King Pelias to cut their father to pieces and boil him, so as to restore his youth. This they did, and in killing him avenged the disgrace of Jason's father Aeson.

Jason and Medea led an unsettled life in Greece. After a few years he deserted her for another woman, but Medea killed this rival and her own children by Jason. Jason died in Corinth as a result of a rotten piece of the *Argo* falling on his head. Afterwards the gods raised the ship to the sky and made it into a constellation. The Golden Fleece also appears in the heavens as the first constellation of the Zodiac, Aries the ram.

ARIADNE, in Greek mythology, was the daughter of *PASIPHAE* and King *MINOS*, the ruler of Knossos on the island of Crete. When the Athenian hero *THESEUS* came to Knossos to pay the annual tribute of seven young men and seven girls, Ariadne gave him a sword and a skein of thread that allowed him to escape from Daedalus' Labyrinth after a bloody struggle with the dreaded bull-headed man, the *MINOTAUR*. Theseus and Ariadne then fled from Crete, but for some unknown reason the hero abandoned the princess on the nearby island of Dia. The deserted princess may then have become the wife of *DIONYSUS*, the god of ecstasy and wine. Local legend would suggest such a connection, although the whole story of the Minotaur was probably no more than a garbled version of far older tales of the sport of bull-leaping, which dated from the pre-Greek era of Cretan history. Dionysus himself was known to the Greeks as "the roaring one", a "bull-horned god" who was full of power and fertility.

ARION see *VOYAGERS*

ARTEMIS was the daughter of the Titaness *LETO* and *ZEUS*, and the twin sister of *APOLLO*. She was in all likelihood a very ancient deity whom the Greeks adopted as goddess of the wild. Traces of human sacrifice could still be found in her worship. Most of all, Artemis liked to roam the mountains with a companion band of nymphs. Certainly the virgin goddess resented any kind of intrusion into her domain, or any harm done to her favourite animals. For killing a stag sacred to Artemis, the leader of the Greek expedition against Troy, King *AGAMEMNON* of Mycenae, found his fleet stranded by contrary winds

at Aulis. Only a promise to sacrifice his daughter *IPHIGENIA* was enough to appease the goddess, although there are differing accounts as to whether the girl was actually killed.

Another mortal punished by Artemis was *ACTAEON*. He had the misfortune while hunting to come upon the goddess as she was bathing. She changed him into a stag and he was chased and torn apart by his own hunting dogs. However, according to a different version, Actaeon actually tried to approach the naked goddess hidden beneath a stag's pelt.

To the Romans, Artemis was closely identified with their goddess Diana, who was also a goddess of light as well as of the wild.

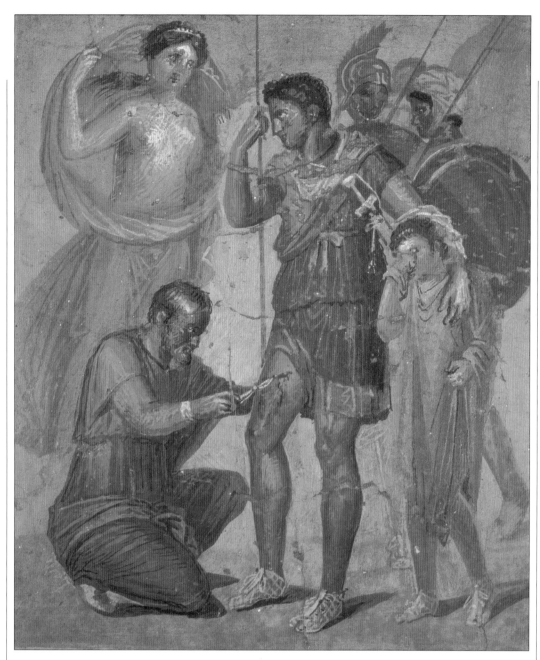

ASCANIUS *weeps beside his wounded father, Aeneas. Close by, in a mantle of mist, Aeneas' divine mother, Venus, descends from heaven with a sprig of healing dittany, while the Greek surgeon, Iapyx, pulls out the arrow-head with his forceps.* (WOUNDED AENEAS, *anon, AD 62 and 79.*)

ASCANIUS was the son of *AENEAS* and Creusa. According to the Romans, he founded the city of Alba Longa thirty-three years after the arrival of the Trojan refugees in Italy. An alternative tradition makes Ascanius' mother Lavinia, a Latin princess whose marriage to Aeneas brought peace and unity to the Latin and Trojan peoples. It was in her honour that Aeneas founded Lavinium within three years of landing. This would mean that Ascanius was king of Lavinium following Aeneas' death, and before he left to take up residence in a new city at Alba Longa. Early rivalry between the two cities probably explains the removal myth.

The family of Julius Caesar, the Julii, claimed descent from Aeneas through Ascanius, who was also called Iulus Ilus ("made of Ilium"), Ilium being the old name for Troy.

ASCLEPIUS, the Greek god of healing, was the son of *APOLLO*, god of prophecy, and the lake nymph Coronis. In mythology he is a somewhat shadowy figure, which suggests his late arrival as a major deity. Asclepius would seem to have been a Thessalian healer whose skills became known throughout Greece: his cult eventually took over the sanctuary at Epidauros in the Peloponnese. Sacred snakes resident there were believed to embody the god's healing power. The ancient association between snakes and medicine is probably due to the snake's apparent ability to renew its youth each year by sloughing off its own skin.

Only the stories of Asclepius' birth and death were ever well known to the Greeks and Romans. When Coronis dared to take in secret a mortal as a second lover, an enraged Apollo sent his sister *ARTEMIS* to kill the lake nymph with a disease. However, as the flames of the funeral pyre burned Coronis, Apollo felt sorry for his unborn son and removed him from the corpse. Thus was Asclepius born. He was taught medicine by the Centaur *CHIRON*, whose knowledge was so great that *ZEUS* himself feared that Asclepius might learn a way of overcoming death. When he did succeed in resurrecting one of his patients, Zeus decided that Asclepius should be punished for threatening the gods' monopoly over immortality. Asclepius was slain by a thunder-bolt, but at Apollo's request the god of medicine was placed among the stars, as Ophiuchus, the serpent-bearer.

So impressed were the Romans with Asclepius' cult that during a time of plague they requested aid from Epidauros and a sacred snake was duly shipped to Rome.

ATALANTA, in Greek mythology, was the daughter of Iasus of Arcadia and was known as a famous huntress. As an unwanted daughter she was exposed and left to die on a mountainside, but was suckled by a bear and later brought up by hunters. This experience may have inclined her to manly pursuits. She even tried to enlist with the *ARGONAUTS*, but *JASON* refused her because the presence of one woman on the ship might cause jealousies amongst them.

Atalanta's most famous myth concerns the lengths to which she went to avoid marriage. She said that her husband must first beat her in a race and any man who lost would be put to death. Despite the awful consequence of losing, there were many who admired Atalanta's beauty and paid the price against her speed. None could catch her, although they ran naked while she was fully clothed. Finally, the love goddess *APHRODITE* took pity on a young man named Melanion and provided him with a way to delay

ASCLEPIUS, Greek god of healing, tends a man on his sickbed. A son of Apollo, the greatest healer, Asclepius was gifted with miraculous powers, once resurrecting a mortal from death. His attributes, staff and serpent, signify power and renewal of life. (ILLUSTRATION BY NICK BEALE, 1995.)

Atalanta. She gave him three golden apples, which he placed at different points on the course. Curiosity got the better of Atalanta, who stopped three times to pick up the apples. So Melanion won the race and Atalanta as a wife. But in his haste to make love to her, Melanion either forgot a vow to Aphrodite or consummated their union in a sacred place. To pay for the sacrilege both he and Atalanta were turned into lions.

ATALANTA, the gifted huntress and unusually athletic heroine, found her match in the equally resourceful and energetic Melanion. Here the heroic pair hunt and slay the monstrous wild boar which has been ravaging the plains of Calydon. (ILLUSTRATION FROM TANGLEWOOD TALES, C. 1920.)

ATHENA, sometimes Athene, the daughter of *ZEUS* and the Titaness Metis, was the Greek goddess of war and crafts. Although a fierce virgin like *ARTEMIS*, she did not shun men but on the contrary delighted in being a city-goddess, most notably at Athens. This city adopted her cult when an olive tree grew on its acropolis: the other divine rival for worship was the god *POSEIDON*, who produced only a spring of brackish water. Athena sprang into being fully grown and armed from the head of her father Zeus, after he had swallowed the pregnant Metis. The smith god *HEPHAISTOS* assisted the birth with a blow from his axe. Quite likely this intervention accounts for her title of Hephaistia, the companion of the smith god. Athena's symbol was the wise owl, which featured on Athenian coins. The Romans identified her with *MINERVA*, a goddess of wisdom and the arts.

An early myth relates how Hephaistos tried to rape Athena. To avoid losing her virginity, she miraculously disappeared so that the semen of the smith god fell to the ground, where it grew into the serpent Erichthonius. The three daughters of Cecrops, the semi-serpent who first ruled Athens, were given a box by Athena and told not to look inside it. Ignoring this command, two of them looked inside, found themselves gazing upon Erichthonius, and went insane. However, Athena continued to protect Athens. Although the city fell into enemy hands during the Persian invasion of Greece in 480–479 BC, the Athenians later went on to achieve mastery of the sea and found their own empire. It was during this period that the Parthenon was built on the Athenian acropolis.

Athena was always regarded by the Greeks as an active goddess, involved in the affairs of men. She helped several heroes such as *BELLEROPHON, JASON, HERACLES* and *PERSEUS*. Also, it was she who eventually got *ODYSSEUS* back to the island of Ithaca, following his epic voyage home from the Trojan War. Perhaps Athena's most significant aid was given to the matricide *ORESTES*. Not only did she offer him protection, but she also arranged for him to be tried and acquitted of his terrible crime by the ancient court of the Areopagus, in Athens. The verdict meant an end to the blood-feud, not least because for the first time even the *FURIES* accepted Orestes' deliverance from guilt.

ATLAS was a *TITAN*, the son of Iapetus and the Oceanid Clymene. He was thought by the ancient Greeks to hold up the sky, and his name means "he who carries". His most famous encounter was with the hero *HERACLES*, one of whose labours was to obtain the golden apples of the *HESPERIDES*, female guardians of the fruit that mother earth, *GAIA*, presented to *HERA* at her marriage to *ZEUS*. Atlas offered to fetch them for Heracles if the

ATHENA, goddess of wisdom and crafts, guided and helped her favourites. Here she visits the hero Bellerophon with a gift – the bridle with which to tame and mount the winged horse, Pegasus. (ILLUSTRATION FROM STORIES FROM GREECE AND ROME, 1930.)

hero took over his job of holding up the sky. When Atlas returned with the apples he suggested that he should deliver them himself, as Heracles was doing so well. The hero pretended to agree and then asked if Atlas would take the world for a moment so that he could adjust the weight on his shoulder, so tricking Atlas into resuming his lonely duty. (See also *GIANTS*)

ATLAS, the great Titan giant, was condemned to shoulder the heavens forever, as punishment for fighting the sky god Zeus. (ILLUSTRATION FROM DICTIONARY OF CLASSICAL ANTIQUITIES, 1891.)

B

ATREUS

ATREUS was the son of *PELOPS*, an early king after whom the Peloponnese in southern Greece is named, and Hippodaemia. The house of Atreus was infamous for the hereditary curse laid upon it by the son of *HERMES*, the messenger god. A terrible cycle of murder and revenge was ended only by the trial in Athens of Atreus' grandson *ORESTES* on a charge of matricide.

Family misfortune stemmed from the action of Pelops, the father of Atreus. He seems either to have brought about the death of Hermes' son Myrtilus, or to have caused him great grief by refusing to make a promised gift. Friction between the sons of Pelops, Atreus, Thyestes and Chrysippus, arose about the ownership of a golden ram, a wondrous animal placed in Atreus' flock by Hermes. First, Chrysippus was murdered by Atreus and Thyestes, then Thyestes seduced Aerope, the wife of Atreus, in order to gain her help in seizing the golden ram. An enraged Atreus slew Aerope and exiled Thyestes.

At a banquet supposedly for reconciliation, Atreus served his brother Thyestes with the flesh of his children. When Thyestes had

ATREUS, son of Pelops, cherished a golden ram, a double-edged gift of the god Hermes. The god gave the coveted treasure to Atreus, hoping to sow strife and discord in the house of Pelops, in revenge for the murder of his son, Myrtilus.
(ILLUSTRATION BY NICK BEALE, 1995.)

BELLEROPHON swoops down for the kill on his winged horse, Pegasus, diving through the smoke and flames of the fire-breathing Chimaera, a monster with the forepart of a lion, the hindpart of a dragon and its middle formed from a goat.
(ILLUSTRATION FROM TANGLEWOOD TALES, C. 1920.)

finished eating, Atreus showed his brother the hands and feet of his dead sons and told him what he had consumed. In horror the sun halted in its course. Thyestes' only surviving son, Aegisthus, may have slain Atreus in revenge for this outrage. Certainly he became the lover of *CLYTEMNESTRA*, whose husband *AGAMEMNON* was the eldest son of Atreus and his successor as king of Mycenae, or Argos. Not until Clytemnestra and Aegisthus had murdered Agamemnon, and were themselves killed by Agamemnon's son *ORESTES*, did the curse of Myrtilus come to an end.

BELLEROPHON

BELLEROPHON was a Greek hero from the city of Corinth and the son of Glaucus. He possessed a wonderful winged horse named *PEGASUS*, which had sprung out of the *GORGON* Medusa's blood when she was beheaded by *PERSEUS*. The goddess *ATHENA* gave Bellerophon a special bridle in order to help him tame Pegasus.

Bellerophon's problems began, as his own name indicates, with a murder. He evidently killed an important Corinthian because in exile he changed his name from Hipponous to Bellerophon ("killer of Bellerus"). Although he was given refuge in Argos by King Proteus, the passion of the local queen Stheneboea for him caused further difficulties, and not least because he steadfastly rejected her advances. Stheneboea accused him of attempted rape and the enraged

BOREAS, one of the four winds, blew from the north, whistling through his conch. He often helped sailors with a friendly breeze. Along with his brother winds, Eurus, Zephyrus and Notus, he was depicted in the Temple of Winds. (ILLUSTRATION FROM DR SMITH'S CLASSICAL DICTIONARY, 1895.)

Proteus dispatched Bellerophon to southern Asia Minor, where he was supposed to meet his end, but service in the local king's forces saved his life. Mounted on Pegasus, the hero was able to overcome the monstrous Chimaera, defeat neighbouring peoples, including the Amazons, and even become the champion of Lycia. A constellation was named after his fabulous winged horse.

Two tales cast a certain shadow over Bellerophon's character. In the first he is credited with a brutal revenge on the false Argive queen. By pretending that he really loved her, Bellerophon persuaded the queen to elope with him on Pegasus, only to push her off the winged horse's back in mid-air. The second tale almost ends in the hero's death when he attempted to fly to Mount Olympus, the home of the gods. *ZEUS* in anger caused Pegasus to unseat Bellerophon, who was lamed for life.

BOREAS

BOREAS, the north wind, was the son of *EOS*, the goddess of dawn, and the Titan Astraeus. His home was thought to be Thrace, which is situated to the north of the Aegean Sea. In contrast to Zephyrus, the

gentle west wind, Boreas was capable of great destruction. During the Persian invasion of Greece, he helped the Greek cause by damaging the Persian fleet at the battle of Artemisium in 480 BC.

Boreas abducted Orithyia, a daughter of King Erechtheus of Attica. Coming across Orithyia dancing near a stream, he then wrapped her up in a cloud and carried her off to Thrace. She bore Boreas twin sons, Calais and Zetes, who were known as the Boreades. At birth these boys were entirely human in appearance, but later they sprouted golden wings from their shoulders. They were killed by the great hero *HERACLES*.

Boreas was worshipped in the city of Athens, where an annual festival, known as the Boreasmi, was celebrated in his honour.

BRITOMARTIS fled from King Minos who pursued her for nine months, until at last, in despair, she leapt into the sea. Luckily, she became entangled in some fishing nets, and when Artemis changed her into a goddess she was known as Dictynna, which means "net". (ILLUSTRATION BY NICK BEALE, 1995.)

BRITOMARTIS ("sweet maid") was said to be the daughter of *ZEUS*. She lived on the island of Crete, where she spent her time as a huntress. King *MINOS* of Knossos tried to make Britomartis his mistress. But she fled from him and in her desperation to preserve her virginity threw herself off a cliff into the sea. The king finally gave up the pursuit when the Cretan goddess sought sanctuary in the sacred grove of *ARTEMIS*, and became her close associate. The myth is almost certainly an account of the amalgamation of two ancient cults.

BRUTUS was said to be the son of Tarquinia, who was the sister of *TARQUINIUS SUPERBUS*. He was the founder of the Roman Republic. Like most Roman myths, the story of Lucius Junius Brutus lays emphasis on duty to the state, even though in this instance it involved the sacrifice of two sons. During the early part of his life Brutus was regarded as a simpleton, which his name implies. Indeed, he was something of a joke in the court of Tarquinius Superbus, the last Etruscan king to rule Rome. When a snake was found in the king's palace, two princes travelled to Delphi to ask the Oracle to explain this event and Brutus accompanied them almost in the role of a jester. The Oracle told the Romans that the first person in the delegation to kiss his mother would be the next ruler of Rome. The princes drew lots to decide who was to kiss their mother on their return home, but Brutus tripped and kissed the earth, much to their amusement.

BRUTUS, the first consul of the new republic of Rome, condemns his sons to death for rising against the government. Brutus, as his name implies, feigned idiocy but was no fool; wisely and dutifully, he led the trial against his rebel sons. (ILLUSTRATION FROM STORIES FROM LIVY, 1885.)

Shortly after their return to Rome, the youngest prince raped *LUCRETIA*, a Roman matron. This act of violation was the last straw for the oppressed Roman aristocracy, especially when it was learned that Lucretia had stabbed herself to death. The outrage was cleverly used by Brutus as a means of overthrowing the monarchy and setting up a republic. The now eloquent Brutus was elected consul, one of the two highest offices of state. But this fulfilment of the Oracle was soon to cause him grief, when a conspiracy to restore Tarquinius Superbus to the throne was found to have the support of Titus and Tiberius, two of Brutus' own sons. As he was the chief magistrate, Brutus, with great dignity, oversaw their arrest, trial and execution. Thus, at the moment of the new Republic's triumph, the typically Roman idea of self-sacrifice appears as part of its foundation myth.

25

C

CACUS see GIANTS

CADMUS was the son of Agenor, king of Phoenicia, and Telephassa, and the brother of EUROPA. When Europa was forcibly taken to Crete by ZEUS, disguised as a bull, Cadmus and his four brothers were sent after her, with instructions not to return home without her. Although the five Phoenician princes failed in their task, they seem to have had an impact on the places where they eventually settled. Cadmus himself was told by the Oracle at Delphi to forget about Europa and instead find a cow with a moon-shaped mark on its flank. He was to follow the animal and build a city on the spot where it chose to lie down and rest. Having found the cow and followed it eastwards to Boeotia, where at last it sank in exhaustion, Cadmus then sent some of his men for water so that they might sacrifice the animal to ATHENA. But these men were attacked by a serpent sprung from the war god ARES. After Cadmus had killed the monster, the goddess Athena advised him to remove its teeth and sow half of them in the ground. Immediately, armed men arose, but wily Cadmus threw stones among them so that, suspecting each other, they fell upon themselves. It was later believed

CADMUS sows the teeth of a dragon he has slain, and instantly the soil bristles with armed warriors, who spring up to attack each other. Only five survived, to become ancestors of the Thebans, whose city Cadmus founded on the site.
(ILLUSTRATION BY NICK BEALE, 1995.)

that the Theban aristocracy was descended from the five warriors who survived the mutual slaughter.

After a period of penance for killing Ares' serpent, Zeus gave Cadmus a wife – none other than Harmonia, the daughter of Ares and APHRODITE, goddess of love. Since he was marrying a goddess, the gods themselves attended the wedding and gave wonderful gifts. The unusual union of mortal and immortal was not blessed by particularly successful offspring, however. One of their descendants, Pentheus, suffered a horrible fate. Having insulted DIONYSUS, he was torn to pieces by the god's female worshippers when he spied on their secret rites. Among the frenzied worshippers was Pentheus' own mother, Agave, the daughter of Cadmus and Harmonia.

The ancient Greeks always acknowledged the importance of Cadmus' reign, hence, his divine wife. He was credited with the introduction from Phoenicia of an alphabet of sixteen letters. There

are in fact a number of ancient accounts of Phoenician activity in the Aegean Sea. For instance, on the island of Cythera, which lies off the southern Peloponnese, a shrine to Aphrodite is known to have been erected based on the goddess's chief temple in Phoenicia.

CALCHAS see ORACLES AND PROPHECIES

CALLISTO see LOVERS OF ZEUS

CASSANDRA was the daughter of PRIAM, king of Troy, and his wife Hecuba. Her beauty was as remarkable as her power of prophecy, which was said to have been a gift from APOLLO, who loved her, but because she refused his advances he condemned her to prophesy the truth but never to be believed.

Cassandra foretold the Trojan War, the true purpose of the Wooden Horse and the murder of

CASSANDRA, frenzied seer, flees through burning Troy, aghast at the sight of her own predictions. Gifted with prophecy, she clearly foresaw the Trojan War and the trickery of the Wooden Horse, but no one believed her for she was fated to be ignored.
(ILLUSTRATION BY NICK BEALE, 1995.)

CERBERUS snarls and growls by the mouth of Hades. A three-headed hound with a snake for a tail, he allowed no shades to return from the dead, though a few slipped by with the help of the gods. His dark den opened onto the Styx along which Charon ferried the dead. (ILLUSTRATION BY GLENN STEWARD, 1995.)

AGAMEMNON, to whom she was awarded as part of his share of the spoils. But ultimately Cassandra had her revenge on the Greeks. When Troy fell, she had sought sanctuary in ATHENA's temple but was raped, and so the goddess punished this sacrilege by killing many of the Greeks during their voyage home. However, Cassandra met her own end at the hands of Agamemnon's wife CLYTEMNESTRA. (See also ORACLES AND PROPHECIES)

CECROPS see FOUNDERS

CENTAURS, according to Greek mythology, were said to be the descendants of IXION, son of ARES. These strange creatures had the head, arms and chest of a man but the legs and lower half of a horse. They lived in Thessaly, fed on meat and were given to riotous behaviour. They were usually depicted as drunken followers of DIONYSUS, except for wise CHIRON who was the tutor to several heroes, including ACHILLES. (See also MONSTERS AND FABULOUS BEASTS)

CERBERUS was a three-headed hound, the offspring of two monsters, TYPHON and Echidna. He was the watchdog of the Greek underworld and stopped anyone trying to return to the land of the living. One of HERACLES' labours was to fetch Cerberus, a challenge the god of the dead, HADES, allowed him to

CHIRON (left) *instructs the youthful Achilles in the arts of war, medicine, hunting, music and prophecy. Unlike his brother Centaurs, who indulged in riotous revelries, Chiron was noted for his wisdom and gentleness.* (THE EDUCATION OF ACHILLES BY POMPEO BATONI, CANVAS, C. 1770.)

CINCINNATUS was a Roman hero who was instrumental in saving the early Republic. In 458 BC, Rome was in danger of being destroyed by the Aequi, a neighbouring Italian tribe. To defeat this threat, the Senate voted to appoint Cincinnatus as dictator, a temporary office vested with unlimited powers. A deputation was sent to his small farm, which was the smallest landholding allowed to qualify for citizenship. The senators found Cincinnatus at work tending his crops. He was told of the Senate's decision and was saluted as dictator. However, the plebeians, the ordinary people, feared that Cincinnatus might abuse his position. Their fears proved groundless and, after the defeat of the Aequi, they voted Cincinnatus a golden wreath at the end of his sixty days of office. He then returned to his fields and was remembered as the perfect example of a virtuous and dutiful Roman citizen.

CINCINATTUS, one of the most modest of Roman heroes and a model of Roman integrity. After 60 days in office, he quietly returned to his farm. (ILLUSTRATION FROM STORIES FROM LIVY, 1885.)

undertake, but only on condition that he was unarmed. Like the *GORGONS*, Cerberus was so dreadful to behold that anyone who looked upon him was turned to stone. He was brother to the Hydra and the Chimaera.

CHIRON was the son of Philyra, daughter of *OCEANOS*, and the Titan *CRONOS*, who had adopted the form of a horse to hide from his wife *RHEA* his passion for Philyra, which is why Chiron had the appearance of a typical *CENTAUR*, with the body and legs of a horse, and the arms and head of a man.

His unusual parentage explains why Chiron was so wise, unlike other Centaurs, for he was learned in music, medicine, hunting and warfare. He was a friend of *APOLLO* and the tutor to several Greek heroes such as *ACHILLES, ASCLEPIUS* and *JASON*. He lived in a cave on Mount Pelion in Thessaly, and when he died *ZEUS* set him in the sky as the constellation Centaurus.

HEROES

THE MYTHS OF ALL CULTURES contain inspiring individuals who express ideal traits and talents, such as the courage of Achilles, might of Heracles, wit of Odysseus and endurance of Oedipus. A classic hero is a champion in every sense, overcoming trials, ridding the world of troublemakers, blazing trails and winning through despite all the odds. Yet he is neither invulnerable nor immortal, though often helped, and sometimes hindered, by the gods. Greek mythology is unusually rich in heroes and heroines of every kind. Some, such as Achilles and Hector, are wartime champions; others, such as Odysseus or Theseus, are heroes for peacetime; some are positive and outgoing, such as Heracles or Perseus; still others are heroes of attitude rather than action, such as Oedipus, Antigone, or Hector, who, at the end, remained steadfast in the face of hopeless defeat.

HERACLES (below) shoots his poisoned arrows at his old foe, the Centaur Nessus, who raced away with his wife, Deianira, while ferrying her across the river Evenus. The dying Centaur offered Deianira the gift of his blood as a salve for preserving the love of Heracles. The love philtre proved to be a fatal trick by which Heracles died many years later, tragically, by the hands of his insecure but loving wife, Deianira, who in her sorrow killed herself. (HERCULES AND NESSUS BY FRANZ VON STUCK, CANVAS 1863-1928.)

HERACLES (above), best known for his mighty labours, was all his life a helper of gods and men, setting the earth free of many monsters and rascals. Worshipped as a hero and deity, he was invoked as a saviour; as the hero of labour and struggle, he was patron deity of the gymnasium. In art he appears as the ideal of manly strength, with massive muscles and grave expression. This celebrated Greek sculpture shows the hero in repose leaning on his club, draped with the famous lion's skin. (THE FARNESE HERCULES BY GLYCON, C. 200 BC.)

ACHILLES (above), godlike hero and peerless warrior was, paradoxically, disguised as a girl in his youth. His divine mother, Thetis, wishing to save him from the Trojan War, hid him amongst the daughters of Lycomedes on Scyros. There Odysseus went, disguised as a merchant, and showed the girls jewels, dresses and arms. Only Achilles seized the arms eagerly, suddenly realizing his true sex and role in life. He then accompanied Odysseus to Troy.
(ODYSSEUS RECOGNISING ACHILLES AFTER FRANS FRANCKEN THE YOUNGER, CANVAS, C. 1570.)

PERSEUS, guided and guarded by the gods, was able to slay the mortal Gorgon, Medusa, one of three frightful sisters who dwelt on the farthest shore of the ocean, and whose looks turned men to stone. By viewing Medusa in his shining shield, Perseus was able to cut off her head as she slept. Hidden by the invisible helmet of Hades he flew to safety on winged sandals given him by the nymphs. Medusa's head was placed on Athena's breastplate – a paralysing power in battle. (ILLUSTRATION FROM TANGLEWOOD TALES, C. 1920.)

CLOELIA (above), Roman heroine, was given as a hostage to the Etruscan, Lars Porsenna, during his campaign against Rome. But she escaped from his camp and swam across the Tiber to Rome. When the Romans sent her back to Porsenna, he was so taken by her gallantry, that he set her free with some other hostages and gave her a splendid horse. Here she rides triumphantly to freedom with her companions. (ILLUSTRATION FROM STORIES FROM LIVY, 1885.)

JASON (above), the celebrated captain of the Argonauts, embarked on a great adventure to bring back the Golden Fleece, which was suspended from a branch of an oak tree in the grove of Ares in Colchis. It was greatly cherished by Aietes, the king of Colchis. With the help of a potion from the sorceress Medea, daughter of the king of Colchis, Jason charmed to sleep the ever-watchful dragon that guarded the Golden Fleece. (ILLUSTRATION FROM TANGLEWOOD TALES, C.1920.)

HORATIUS (above), brave Roman hero, held the Sublician Bridge with two comrades against the Etruscan army. While he held off the Etruscans, the Romans hacked the bridge behind him until it collapsed. Having sent back his comrades, Horatius stood alone until the bridge fell, then he swam to safety across the raging Tiber, amid enemy arrows. The state erected a statue to his honour in the Comitium. (ILLUSTRATION FROM LAYS OF ANCIENT ROME, 1891.)

CIRCE (left), an enchanting nymph, invites Odysseus to drink from her magic cup, containing a potion which turns men into swine. But Odysseus has been forewarned and, immunized with the herb moly, he drinks without coming to harm. (ILLUSTRATION FROM TANGLEWOOD TALES, C.1920.)

CLYTEMNESTRA (above), the estranged wife of Agamemnon, watches and waits for the ships from Troy, bringing her husband home. Yet no hero's welcome awaits the returning warrior, only betrayal and murder by his wife and her lover. (ILLUSTRATION BY NICK BEALE, 1995.)

CIRCE, daughter of *HELIOS*, the sun god, was a powerful witch who had poisoned her husband, king of the Sarmatians, before going to the fabulous island of Aeaea. Her magical powers turned *ODYSSEUS'* men into swine when they landed on Aeaea on their way home from Troy. Aided by *HERMES*, the messenger god, Odysseus was immune to Circe's magic and restored his crew to human form, and also gained the witch's aid for the next part of his journey. For a year he stayed as her lover, before she told him how to navigate through the waters of the Sirens and between Scylla, a monster, and Charybdis, a whirlpool. Scylla had been a rival of Circe, who had turned her into a monster when one of her many lovers had shown an interest in the unfortunate girl. In some accounts, Circe eventually married Odysseus' son Telemachus.

CLOELIA see *HEROES*

CLYTEMNESTRA was the daughter of *LEDA* and Tyndareos, king of Sparta, and the estranged wife of *AGAMEMNON*. Sometimes she is portrayed as a weak woman, easily persuaded by her lover Aegisthus to assist in the murder of her husband on his return from the Trojan War. Otherwise it is Clytemnestra who is the strong character, the instigator of the murder, while Aegisthus is little more than a weakling. Even before the the Greek force departed for Troy, Clytemnestra already had good reason to hate her husband. In order to gain a fair wind to Troy, he agreed to sacrifice her favourite child *IPHIGENIA*. Even though the champion *ACHILLES* had promised to defend the girl against all threats, the Greek host had its way and Iphigenia was offered to the goddess *ARTEMIS*, either as sacrificial victim or as priestess.

Like her sister *HELEN*, whose elopement with *PARIS* caused the Trojan War, Clytemnestra felt no loyalty towards her husband. She openly conducted an affair with Aegisthus, Agamemnon's cousin, and ruled Mycenae with him. The end of the war required desperate measures. When he returned home Agamemnon was butchered by Aegisthus, using a two-headed axe, while Clytemnestra had him entangled in a net. For this terrible crime, Clytemnestra was herself killed by her son *ORESTES*.

CORIOLANUS was a legendary Roman traitor of the fifth century BC. Conscious above all of his noble birth, Coriolanus objected to the Senate's wish to distribute free bread to poorer citizens, who were starving because of Rome's endless wars. He said that unless the plebeians, the ordinary people, were willing to restore to the nobility its full ancient privileges they should expect no charity. Hounded from Rome for such an opinion, he joined the Volsci and eventually led a Volscian army against the city. All seemed lost until his mother Volumnia spoke to him, asking Coriolanus whether he saw her as his own mother or as a prisoner of war. As a result he quit the battlefield and went into exile.

CREON, in Greek mythology, was the brother of Jocasta and a reluctant ruler of Thebes. He was regent during the uncertain period after King *LAIUS*, Jocasta's husband, had been killed near the city. Creon offered the throne and the hand of Jocasta to any man who could solve the riddle of the *SPHINX* and thus rid Thebes of this bloodthirsty

CREON, reluctant king of Thebes, lost his son, wife and niece in a tragic cycle of suicides caused by his inflexible will. His crushing fate was to endure a life of solitary grief and remorse. (ILLUSTRATION BY NICK BEALE, 1995.)

CORIOLANUS, a Roman exile, marched against his old city with an army of Volscians, encamping just outside Rome. There, he ignored all entreaties for peace until visited by his mother (centre), his wife and the Roman matrons, whose tears softened his stern heart. (ILLUSTRATION FROM STORIES FROM LIVY, 1885.)

monster. *OEDIPUS* managed to achieve the apparently impossible task, then took over the kingdom, married Jocasta and raised a family. Not until a plague threatened Thebes and the Delphic Oracle was consulted about its cause, did it become known that Jocasta was Oedipus' mother and that he had killed Laius. Oedipus blinded himself, Jocasta committed suicide and Creon became regent once more.

A quarrel between Oedipus' sons, Eteocles and Polynices, caused another period of dismay, eventually leaving both of them dead and Creon on the throne. Whereas Eteocles was regarded by Creon as a patriot and properly buried, the body of the rebel Polynices was thrown outside the city walls and forbidden burial. Such a situation was unacceptable to *ANTIGONE*, Oedipus' daughter and companion during his wanderings around Greece, and on her return to Thebes she sprinkled Polynices' corpse with earth, so as to give her brother a token burial.

As a result of this act of defiance, Creon had Antigone walled up in a cave. The seer *TIRESIAS* told Creon to bury the dead and disinter the living, but he refused. The result was personal grief, when his own son committed suicide on learning of Antigone's death, and his own wife soon followed suit.

Although Creon was well known to the ancient Greeks, his own character seems less important in myth than his role as regent in the troubled city of Thebes.

CRONOS, in Greek mythology, was the son of Ouranos, the sky god, and *GAIA*, the earth mother. With the help of Gaia, Cronos emasculated Ouranos and seized control of the universe. He then married his sister *RHEA* and followed the example of Ouranos in disposing of his children by swallowing them, because he had been warned that he would be displaced by one of his sons. Rhea, however, gave him a stone wrapped in swaddling clothes instead of the infant *ZEUS*, his youngest son, who was taken secretly to Crete in order to grow up safely on the island. When Zeus came of age, he forced Cronos to vomit up his brothers and sisters – *POSEIDON, HADES, HERA, HESTIA* and *DEMETER* – and to release his uncles and aunts, especially the Titans, whom Cronos had chosen

to keep chained up. In gratitude, the Cyclopes, the single-eyed giants, fashioned for Zeus his famous lightning and thunderbolts.

In a subsequent struggle for power, Zeus and his brothers successfully dealt with all the might and power that Cronos could direct against them. After his defeat, Cronos was either banished to a distant paradise, or he simply slowly faded away as an unimportant deity. The Romans equated Cronos with their *SATURN*, who

was a corn god whom they associated with the Golden Age.

CUPID was the Roman god of love and son of the love goddess *VENUS*. He was depicted as a beautiful but wanton boy, armed with a quiver full of "arrowed desires". Some of his arrows, however, would turn people away from those who fell in love with them.

According to one myth, Venus was jealous of *PSYCHE* ("the soul") and told Cupid to make her love the ugliest man alive. But Cupid fell in love with Psyche and, invisible, visited her every night. He told her not to try to see him, but, overcome by curiosity, she did try and he left her. Psyche searched the world for him, until the sky god *JUPITER* granted her immortality so that she could be Cupid's constant companion. The couple's daughter was named Voluptas ("pleasure").

CUPID fishes playfully amongst the waves. He is usually portrayed as a cute, capricious child with wings and often with a quiver of arrows or a torch to inflame love in the hearts of gods and men. (CUPID FISHING BY GEORGE FREDERICK WATTS, SEPIA C. 1890.)

D

CURTIUS

CURTIUS is the subject of a strange incident in Roman mythology. Around 362 BC a great chasm appeared in the Forum in Rome, which led straight down to the underworld. It had appeared because the Romans forgot to make an appropriate sacrifice to the dead. Marcus Curtius therefore plunged on horseback into the bottomless pit and was seen no more.

CYCLOPES see GIANTS

DAEDALUS, according to Greek mythology, was said by some to be the son of Alcippe, the daughter of the war god ARES, and by others to be the son of Merope. It is agreed, though, that he came from Athens. He was a gifted craftsman and was employed by King MINOS at his palace of Knossos in Crete. Daedalus designed and built the Labyrinth for the dreaded MINOTAUR. This was the offspring of PASIPHAE, Minos' wife, and a great bull. Daedalus had designed an artificial cow into which the queen could place herself and so be able to mate with the bull. Thus was the Minotaur conceived. Minos later imprisoned Daedalus for revealing the secret of the Labyrinth, but he managed to escape by constructing

DAPHNE, a river nymph, was loved by Apollo who pursued her until, on the banks of her father's river, she prayed for help and was at once changed into a laurel tree. Here, her father, the river god Peneius, weeps inconsolably, while Apollo strokes her leafy arms in wonder. (APOLLO AND DAPHNE BY NICOLAS POUSSIN, CANVAS, C.1627)

wings of wax and feathers for himself and his son Icarus. Despite his father's warning, Icarus flew too close to the sun, the wax of his wings melted and he fell into the sea and drowned. Daedalus managed to arrive safely in Sicily, where he amused the daughters of King Cocalos with his inventions. When Minos eventually caught up with the fugitive craftsman, a battle of wits ended in Daedalus' favour: Minos was killed by boiling water, or oil, which Daedalus persuaded Cocalos' daughters to pour down a pipe into the king's bath.

DANAE was the mother of the Greek hero PERSEUS and the daughter of Acrisius, king of Argos in the Peloponnese. It had been foretold that her son would cause the death of Acrisius, so he locked her in a bronze tower. But ZEUS visited her as a shower of golden rain and Perseus was conceived. The king banished the mother and her son, but after many adventures Perseus did accidentally kill Acrisius when throwing a discus. (See also LOVERS OF ZEUS)

DANAE (above) was imprisoned in a bronze tower by her father, because he feared a prophecy that he would be killed by his grandson. Yet even hidden away in her tower, she was still accessible to the god Zeus, who came to her as a golden shower. They had a son, Perseus. (DANAE AND THE GOLDEN RAIN BY TITIAN, CANVAS, 1554.)

DAEDALUS (right) crafted wings of feathers, held together by wax, to escape from Crete, and taught his son, Icarus, how to fly, warning him that he must not fly too close to the sun. But Icarus was drawn to the light of the sun, so his wings melted and he fell into the sea, now named the Icarian. (DAEDALUS AND ICARUS BY CHARLES LANDON, 1799.)

DAPHNE, in Greek mythology, was the daughter of the river god Peneius. She was similar in many ways to the goddess ARTEMIS, in that she was also a virgin huntress who happily roamed the wilderness. One day, the love god EROS shot a flurry of arrows in response to taunts from APOLLO, the god of prophecy. The first of Eros' arrows was a gold-tipped shaft and when it struck Apollo it made him fall immediately in love with Daphne. The second one, however, had a lead tip and caused Daphne to become even more indifferent than she already had been to any lover. Apollo, however, pursued Daphne relentlessly until, in desperation, she turned herself into a laurel tree

DEMETER, (left) goddess of the earth, and her daughter, Persephone, holding a mystic torch, consecrate the young Triptolemus, the first man to sow corn. This relief was found at Eleusis, site of the Eleusian mysteries which centred on Demeter and her worship. (MARBLE RELIEF, C. 490 BC.)

dead she pined and refused to eat any food, while in the world of the living her mother lost all interest in fertility, so that plants languished, animals ceased to multiply and people feared for their future. Eventually, Zeus had to intervene and rule that Hades must give up Persephone if she would not consent to stay with him. As she had by then eaten something in his realm, it was deemed that she had not completely rejected Hades, so henceforth Persephone would divide the year equally between her mother and her husband.

DIDO (below), exotic queen of Carthage, tragically stabbed herself when her lover Aeneas deserted her to fulfil his destiny, and lead his people to Rome. The heroine is portrayed by Virgil as a noble and generous soul who, in the classic tradition, endures her tragic fate alone.
(ILLUSTRATION BY NICK BEALE, 1995.)

DELPHIC ORACLE see
ORACLES AND PROPHECIES

DEMETER, the Greek goddess of vegetation and fruitfulness, was the daughter of *CRONOS* and *RHEA*. Like her Roman equivalent, Ceres, she was especially associated with corn. Demeter possessed mysterious powers of growth and even resurrection. She was the focus of an important cult at Eleusis, just south of Athens, where rites were celebrated annually in the autumn when, through music and dancing, her worshippers recalled the loss and rediscovery of her daughter *PERSEPHONE*. Demeter means "mother earth" – the abundant soil as well as the resting-place of the dead (which were known by the Athenians as "Demeter's people").

Her myth turns on the disappearance of Persephone. When the girl was a child, her father, *ZEUS*, without even consulting Demeter, agreed to his brother *HADES'* request that Persephone should be his bride and rule the underworld with him. Hades was impatient and rose from the earth and abducted Persephone as she plucked flowers in a field. But in the world of the

The story of Demeter and Persephone is clearly ancient. It has parallels in the mythology of West Asia, where growth and decay were closely associated with a dying and reviving deity. For the Greeks, Persephone as Kore ("the maiden"), was identified as the power within the corn itself, which was a natural extension of her mother the corn goddess Demeter.

DIONYSUS was the son of *ZEUS* and *SEMELE*, who was a Theban princess. In Greek mythology, he is a youthful god of vegetation, wine and ecstasy, known as the "bull-horned god" because he often adopted the form of this powerful beast. In Roman mythology he is represented by the god Bacchus. Originally, he may have had a mythological role somewhat similar to that of the goddess *DEMETER* ("mother earth"). His cult in later times, however, developed into one of personal salvation, particularly for women worshippers who were known as maenads.

From the beginning, the ancient Greeks were well aware of the strange character of Dionysus, and in some city-states his wild, orgiastic rites were outlawed. The most famous attempt to prohibit his worship was by King Pentheus of Thebes. The king even tried to imprison Dionysus, but the chains fell off him and the prison doors could not be closed. Dionysus then told Pentheus that he could observe at first hand the secret rituals performed on a mountain close to the city, but only if he disguised himself as a woman. The king readily took the bait and spied on the maenads from a hiding-place in a tree. However, the maenads soon discovered him and, in their ecstatic frenzy, thought that he was a lion and tore him limb from limb. Afterwards his mother, Agave, who was also one of the leading maenads, realized to her horror that they had dismembered not a lion but her son. After his burial, Agave, together with her parents, *CADMUS* and Harmonia, left Thebes and went into exile. (See also *LOVERS OF ZEUS*)

DIDO, originally a princess of Tyre, in Phoenicia, became the tragic queen of Carthage and the abandoned love of *AENEAS*. Her husband had been murdered by her brother, when the latter ascended the throne of Tyre. Dido escaped from Phoenicia with a small band of followers and settled in present-day Tunisia, where she purchased enough land to found the city of Carthage. The local ruler agreed to sell her as much ground as a bull's hide might contain, so Dido cut the skin into strips in order to obtain an adequate plot.

When the Trojan hero Aeneas arrived in Carthage, having been blown off course on his way to Italy from Troy, Dido welcomed him and his fellow refugees with great understanding. Aeneas and Dido soon fell in love, but the Roman god *JUPITER* sent *MERCURY* with a message reminding Aeneas of his destiny to found a new Troy in Italy and ordering him to resume his voyage at once. When Aeneas sailed away, Dido became so overwhelmed by the loss of her lover that she stabbed herself and then leapt into the flames of a pyre. (See also *FOUNDERS*)

E

THE DIOSCURI, the mysterious twin sons of *LEDA*, queen of Sparta, were known to the Greeks as Castor and Polydeuces, and to the Romans as Castor and Pollux. They were brothers of *HELEN* and *CLYTEMNESTRA*. Around all these children, except Clytemnestra, there hung a definite sense of divine parentage, and it may well be that they were ancient deities whose worship had declined so that their exploits could be told as the mythological actions of mortal rulers. Castor and Polydeuces ("the heavenly twins whom the corn-bearing earth holds") were regarded as being both dead and alive. In one story, Polydeuces was the immortal son of *ZEUS* while Castor was the mortal son of King Tyndareos. At Polydeuces' request the twins shared the divinity between them, living half the year beneath the earth with the dead, and the other half on Mount Olympus with the gods. They are shown together in the constellation of Gemini.

In their youth the Dioscuri ("the sons of Zeus") were *ARGONAUTS*. During the expedition to retrieve the Golden Fleece, Polydeuces killed with his bare hands Amycus, king of the savage Bebryces, who were a people living in Asia Minor. On another occasion the twins were ranged against the Athenian hero *THESEUS*, who carried off the twelve-year-old Helen prior to her marriage to King *MENELAUS*. They brought their sister safely home to Sparta, and even set up a rival to Theseus on the throne of Athens.

THE DIOSCURI (above), twins Castor and Pollux, returned to earth to help the Roman ranks against the Latins in the fabled Battle of Lake Regillus. Adorned with gleaming armour, and mounted on snow-white steeds, they led the Romans to victory. *(ILLUSTRATION FROM LAYS OF ANCIENT ROME, 1881.)*

The Dioscuri were revered by the Spartans and the Romans in particular. Roman soldiers swore that the presence of Castor and Pollux on a battlefield secured for them victories against all the odds.

ELECTRA was the daughter of *AGAMEMNON*, king of Mycenae, and *CLYTEMNESTRA*, and the sister of the matricide *ORESTES*. Her name (which once may have meant "fire" or "spark") refers to amber. When Agamemnon returned from the Trojan War and was murdered by his wife and her lover Aegisthus, Electra rescued her young brother Orestes and ensured that he escaped Aegisthus' evil intentions. Years later, Orestes returned to Mycenae as a grown man. Electra met him at the tomb of their murdered father and gave him advice and encouragement. In at least one version of the myth Electra is portrayed as being so consumed by hatred for Clytemnestra that she participates in the act of revenge herself. Later she was overwhelmed by remorse, while her distraught brother fled before the *FURIES*, the deities who wreaked vengeance on murderers.

ENDYMION was the king of a small city-state in the Peloponnese,

ELECTRA (above), heroic daughter of Agamemnon and Clytemnestra, meets her exiled brother Orestes outside Agamemnon's tomb. It was Electra who rescued her brother from the evil intentions of Aegisthus by helping him escape. Having thought that she would never see him again, she is seen here rejoicing in his return. (ORESTE AND ELECTRA, MARBLE, C. AD 100.)

EOS (below), Greek goddess of the dawn, rises early each day to announce the coming of the sun. She was the daughter of Hyperion and Theia and sister to the sun god Helios. In works of art, she is often depicted hovering in the sky, her rosy form adorned in a golden mantle. She is accompanied here by her starry daughters. *(ILLUSTRATION FROM STORIES FROM HOMER, 1885.)*

ENDYMION (above) was loved by Selene who visited him in his eternal sleep. Here, the lovers part at dawn. In the sky, the goddess sprinkles dew before the sun-chariot, while on earth Nyx draws a curtain of darkness about her. (SELENE AND ENDYMION BY NICOLAS POUSSIN, CANVAS, C. 1594-1665.)

EUROPA (right) was a Phoenician princess borne away by Zeus, who assumed the form of a great white bull. He swam to the island of Crete with Europa riding on his back. She eventually married Asterius, the ruler of Crete. (ILLUSTRATION FROM DR SMITH'S CLASSICAL DICTIONARY, 1895.)

in all likelihood Elis. According to Greek mythology, he became the lover of the moon goddess Selene (frequently identified with Diana), who bore him fifty daughters. Because she could not endure the thought that Endymion would eventually die, Selene put her youthful lover into an everlasting, deep sleep. However, in another version of the myth, it is said that ZEUS granted Endymion his wish that he might be allowed to sleep forever in a cave without ageing

EOS was the Greek, winged goddess of the dawn and the third child of the TITANS Hyperion and

Theia. She was seen as a charioteer riding across the sky just before sunrise, pulled by her horses Shiner and Bright. Her brother, the sun god HELIOS, had a four-horse chariot to indicate his greater status. The Romans called her Aurora.

Eos had a reputation for passion and fell in love with a large number of young men, including the particularly handsome Tithonus, son of Laomedon, king of Troy. When Eos asked ZEUS to make Tithonus immortal, she forgot about eternal youth and ended with a lover made helpless with age. Thereupon, according to different versions of the myth, she

locked him in a bedchamber or he became the cicada (an insect noted for its complaining sound).

ERINYES see FURIES

EROS, according to some Greek traditions, was the son of Erebos and the Night, while in others he was the son of ARES, god of war. As the youngest of the gods and the companion of APHRODITE, he appeared to enjoy making as much mischief as he could by firing his arrows of passion into the hearts of gods and humans alike. His connection with homosexual love may have derived from his supposed

relationship to Ares, for he was the patron divinity of the Sacred Band of Thebes, which was a group of one hundred and fifty pairs of lovers who were all killed by the Macedonian army at the battle of Chaeronia in 338 BC. After the battle King Philip of Macedon granted them a special burial.

EUROPA, in Greek mythology, was the daughter of Telephassa and of King Agenor of Tyre, a city in Phoenicia. Agenor's five sons, including CADMUS, were sent out to look for their sister after ZEUS, disguised as a white bull, swam to the island of Crete with Europa on his back. There she bore the god three sons, MINOS, RHADAMANTHYS and SARPEDON, before marrying the local ruler Asterius. By way of compensation for Europa's virginity, Zeus gave Asterius a mighty bronze man, Talos, to defend his realm. (See also LOVERS OF ZEUS)

ORACLES AND PROPHECIES

IN THE ANCIENT WORLD, a man's life was thought to be determined by fate or destiny. Even the gods themselves were, to a large extent, subject to fate, although it was Zeus who saw to it that fate took its proper course. As people believed that the future could be revealed, they frequently consulted oracles of every kind for personal and political purposes. The most famous was the Delphic Oracle where Apollo, the seer-god, spoke through a priestess. The future was also revealed by oracular signs, such as the fall of dice, lots, or burnt offerings. Dreams afforded another type of oracle, usually inspired by the gods, sometimes to mislead. Prophecies were also sought from seers, both living and dead. Although the Romans consulted lots (or sortes) for personal problems, they rarely, if ever, prophesied for political purposes.

DREAMS (below) could sometimes reveal the future and were often inspired by the gods, usually to guide a favourite mortal in distress. Here, Penelope is visited in her dream by Athena in the form of her sister Iphthime. The vision consoled Penelope in her troubles and predicted that her son, Telemachus, though in grave danger, would nonetheless return home safely. (ILLUSTRATION FROM STORIES FROM HOMER, 1885.)

CASSANDRA (above), fairest daughter of Priam and Hecuba, was a gifted but tragic seer, who was doomed to be ignored. She was endowed with prophecy by Apollo, in exchange for the promise of her love. When she broke her word, he punished her by decreeing that her prophecies, however true, would always be ignored. This powerful portrayal of Cassandra reveals the solitary, all-seeing world of the sorrowful seer, who accurately predicted the fall of Troy. (CASSANDRA BY MAX KLINGER, MARBLE, 1886-95.)

THE DELPHIC ORACLE (left), ancient and fabled seat of prophecy at Delphi, was described as the "navel of the earth". The oracle itself was a cleft in the ground which emitted cold vapours, inducing ecstasy. Over the chasm the seer sat on a gilded tripod inhaling the vapours and uttering enigmatic words which were recorded by a priest and interpreted as the revelations of Apollo. (ILLUSTRATION FROM TANGLEWOOD TALES, C. 1920.)

THE FATES (above), or Moerae, spun out a child's destiny at birth, symbolized by a thread which was drawn, measured and cut off. Although Greek portrayals of the spinners reveal grave, busy maidens, the Romantic Fatae can seem mean, denying humans their hopes and desires. Here they appear as frightful old hags: Clotho, on the left, unravels a spindle in the shape of a helpless child, while Lachesis squints through her glass and Atropos manically waves her scissors. The fourth figure possibly symbolizes the general concept of destiny. (THE FATES BY FRANCISCO DE GOYA, CANVAS, 1819-23.)

SIGNS OR OMENS (below) foretold the future in a variety of ways. Sometimes lots or dice were thrown; sometimes burnt offerings were inspected at the altar. In some sacred precincts, the sound of a rustling oak or the clash of cymbals signified a response to the seeker's question. Here, offerings are burnt at the altar, and examined for signs of the future. (ILLUSTRATION FROM STORIES FROM HOMER, 1885.)

CALCHAS (above), celebrated seer, accompanied the Greeks on their expedition against Troy, correctly predicting that the Trojan war would last ten years. It was prophesied that he would die when he met a seer wiser than himself, and when the soothsayer, Mopsus, beat him in a match of guessing riddles, Calchas died of grief. A temple was erected to him in Apulia where the votaries received oracles in their sleep. (THE SACRIFICE OF IPHIGENIA BY GIOVANNI BATTISTA, TEMPERA, 1770.)

G

THE FATES, or the Moerae, were invoked at birth to decide a man's destiny. Often depicted as spinners, Clotho, at the right, with a spindle spins out the thread of life, while Lachesis, at the left, measures the length of a life, and Atropos, with the shears, cuts it off. (A GOLDEN THREAD BY J M STRUDWICK, OIL ON CANVAS, C. 1890.)

THE FATES, from the Roman, Fatae, were three goddesses known to the Greeks as the Moerae. Their origins are uncertain, although some called them daughters of night. It is clear, however, that at a certain period they ceased to be concerned with death and became instead those powers which decided what must happen to individuals. The Greeks knew them as Clotho ("the spinner"), Lachesis ("the apportioner") and Atropos ("the inevitable"). A late idea was that the Fates spun a length of yarn which represented the allotted span for each mortal.

Although *ZEUS* was the chief Greek god, he was still subject to the decisions of the Fates, and thus the executor of destiny rather than its source. Hence the great importance to both gods and humans of oracles which indicated the inevitable drift of events. In mythology, however, the Fates played little direct part. (See also *ORACLES AND PROPHECIES*)

FAUNUS was the Roman god of the countryside and identified with the Greek *PAN,* god of the mountainside. Faunus was said to be the grandson of *SATURN* and was credited with prophetic powers, which on occasion inspired the Romans to renew efforts on the battlefield in the face of defeat. Perhaps this is the reason for Faunus sometimes

FAUNUS, a spirit of the plains and fields, frolics along with a friendly goat. Faunus' children, known as Fauni, half-men, half-goats, were delightful but capricious creatures, who sometimes plagued men's sleep with nightmares. (ILLUSTRATION FROM DR SMITH'S CLASSICAL DICTIONARY, 1895.)

being seen as a descendant of the war god *MARS*. His mortal son, Latinus, was the king of the Latin people at the time of *AENEAS'* arrival in Italy after the long voyage from Troy.

FLORA see *FORCES OF NATURE*

THE FURIES, from the Roman name, Furiae, were the avenging goddesses of Greek mythology and were known as the Erinyes ("the angry ones"). They were born from the blood of Ouranos that fell into the womb of *GAIA*, when *CRONOS,* his son, castrated him. The Furies

A FURY, goddess of punishment, wields a torch, scourge and spears – the tools of her vengeance. The Furies pursued without mercy in life and in death all wrong-doers. Sometimes they were winged, symbolizing the swiftness of their vengeance. (ILLUSTRATION FROM DR SMITH'S CLASSICAL DICTIONARY, 1895.)

were portrayed as ugly women with snakes entwined in their hair, and were pitiless to those mortals who had wrongly shed blood. They relentlessly pursued *ORESTES*, who avenged his father *AGAMEMNON*'s murder by killing *CLYTEMNESTRA*, his mother. The Furies were only persuaded to abandon their persecution of Orestes after his acquittal by the Areopagus, an ancient Athenian council presided over by the goddess *ATHENA*. The verdict calmed the anger of the Furies, whose name was then changed to the less-threatening Eumenides, ("the soothed ones").

GAIA, in Greek mythology, was the earth, who came out of Chaos and gave birth to Ouranos the sky god, who was her son and husband. So passionate was their relationship and so overwhelming Ouranos' embrace that their offspring could not emerge from her womb. One of these buried children, *CRONOS*, the youngest son, decided to overthrow Ouranos. Gaia conceived a great sickle which Cronos used to cut off his father's penis within the earth womb. The god was emasculated and the sky separated from the earth. From Ouranos' blood, Gaia conceived the *FURIES*, the avenging goddesses who pursued murderers.

Ouranos then faded from the mythological scene and Cronos ruled the universe, taking his sister *RHEA* as a wife. The Greeks regarded this as the golden age of the *TITANS*. Cronos, however, turned out to be as tyrannical to his own family as Ouranos had been before him. He had been warned by an oracle that he would be displaced by one of his sons, so he swallowed his children as soon as they were born. Rhea, on Gaia's advice, gave him a stone wrapped in swaddling instead of the infant *ZEUS*, who was secretly taken to Crete in order to grow up there in safety. When Zeus was grown, he compelled his father to disgorge his brothers and sisters, including his future wife *HERA*, the sea god *POSEIDON*, the god of the underworld *HADES* and *DEMETER*, the goddess of vegetation.

Gaia may have saved Zeus from a fate similar to that of Ouranos and Cronos when she warned him that a child of his born by Metis

GAIA, the great earth mother, pushes through the fruitful earth with her gifts of fertility and abundance. Not only was she the mother of all and the nourisher of children, but she was also a goddess of death who, like the earth, calls her creatures back to her. (ILLUSTRATION BY NICK BEALE, 1995.)

("thought") would replace him as the supreme god. So Zeus swallowed Metis and later the goddess *ATHENA* sprang from his head.

The story of the separation between sky and earth is an ancient one. It is found in a variety of forms in West Asian mythology. The Hurrians, who lived on the borders of modern Turkey and Iraq, had in their myths the most violent version of the sky's emasculation. Kumarbi, the equivalent of Cronos, bit off and swallowed his father's penis. As a result of his unusual action, however, Kumarbi became pregnant with terrible deities, one of whom at last overthrew him.

GANYMEDE, in Greek mythology, was the son of Tros, the king of Phrygia, and brother of Ilus. He was such a beautiful young man that *ZEUS* abducted him and took him to Mount Olympus to be his cupbearer. It was believed that Ganymede also became Zeus' lover, and gained his immortality as the constellation Aquarius, the water-carrier.

GANYMEDE, a handsome boy, excited the passion of Zeus who, in the guise of an eagle, bore him away to Mount Olympus.
(THE RAPE OF GANYMEDE, BY PETER PAUL RUBENS, CANVAS, 1577-1640.)

HADES (above), lord of the underworld, with his wife, Persephone, receives the souls of the dead, who are guided by Hermes. Hades appears with typically dark looks and unruly hair over which he often wore a magic helmet. (ILLUSTRATION FROM DR SMITH'S CLASSICAL DICTIONARY, 1895.)

HECTOR (below), the Trojan champion, snatches a moment of peace with his loving wife and small son. He was portrayed as both a raging warrior and a gentle family man who had taught himself to be valiant out of duty rather than any natural courage. (ILLUSTRATION BY ALAN LEE, 1994.)

THE GIANTS (above) were gigantic creatures with snake-like tails. After they were defeated by the gods, they were buried beneath volcanoes. Here we see the hound of Artemis killing a giant at the battle of the Giants and the gods. (ZEUS ALTAR OF PERGAMON, MARBLE, C. 180 BC.)

THE GIANTS, from the Roman name, Gigantes, in Greek mythology, had human shape, except for the snake-like tails that were attached to their legs. They were born at the same time as the *FURIES*, from the blood that fell into *GAIA's* womb from Ouranos' severed penis. When the Giants attacked Olympus, the gods stood their ground, but knew that they would not be able to defeat them, because the Giants could not be killed by divine hands. *ZEUS* therefore fathered the great hero *HERACLES* through a mortal woman. During the great battle between the gods and the Giants, Heracles played a decisive part, finishing off each opponent with poisoned arrows. It is important to realize that the Giants are quite different from the *TITANS*, who were the oldest generation of the gods and were led by *CRONOS*, Zeus' father.

THE GORGON MEDUSA (above) was once a beautiful woman whose locks were turned to writhing snakes by a vengeful goddess. The image of her frightful face was carved, like an evil eye, on warriors' shields, city walls, charms and amulets. (ILLUSTRATION FROM DR SMITH'S CLASSICAL DICTIONARY, 1895.)

THE GORGONS were three sisters named Stheno ("strength"), Medusa ("queen") and Euryale ("wide-leaping"), and were the children of Phorcys, son of *GAIA*. The only mortal of the three was Medusa, the victim of the Greek hero *PERSEUS*. Like her immortal sisters, she had snakes for hair and one look at her face could turn any living man or thing to stone.

THE GRACES, from the Roman name, Gratiae, were the daughters of *ZEUS* and Eurynome, and were minor goddesses to both the Greeks and the Romans. According to the most widely accepted myth, their names were Aglaia, Euphrosyne and Thalia. They were attendants to *APHRODITE* and *VENUS*, the love goddesses of Greece and Rome respectively. A favourite subject for artists, the Graces were thought to represent beauty, gentleness and friendship.

*THE GRACES, or Charities, graced the world with beauty, bloom and brilliance, lifting the spirits of gods and men. In the earliest works of art, the Graces appear in flowing chitons, veiling their beauty, but later on they were depicted as nudes. (*THE THREE GRACES *BY RAPHAEL, WOOD, C. 1501.)*

HADES (whose name means "the unseen") was the Greek god of the underworld, the realm of the dead. He was the son of *CRONOS* and *RHEA*, and the brother of *ZEUS, POSEIDON, HERA, DEMETER* and Hestia. He forcibly married *PERSEPHONE*, Demeter's daughter. At the division of the universe after the overthrow of their father, Zeus took the sky, Poseidon the sea, and Hades the underworld; the earth was to be shared among them. Another name for Hades was Polydegmon ("receiver of many guests") on account of the multitudes who had died and come to his kingdom. The ghosts of the dead were escorted by *HERMES*, the messenger god, to the boatman Charon who ferried across the Styx, a subterranean river, only those ghosts who could pay the fare. *CERBERUS*, the three-headed dog, guarded the entrance to the underworld and prevented anyone from returning to the world of the living.

As in Egyptian mythology, the Greeks associated the underworld with the west, the place where the sun sets. Neither the Greeks nor the Romans, however, ever thought of Hades as an evil force like Satan in Christianity. He was certainly a grim and implacable deity, and worshippers always averted their eyes when making a sacrifice. In order to avoid any reference to the nature of the underworld it was usual to call Hades by the title of Pluto ("the giver of wealth").

Hades' chief myth concerns the abduction of Persephone, who was the daughter of Demeter and his brother Zeus. Persephone was abruptly taken underground by Hades when she beheld a special narcissus planted by the earth mother *GAIA* to please the god of death. The conflict between Hades and Demeter over Persephone's fate was decided by Zeus, who gave the husband and the mother equal shares of her time. As a dying-and-rising goddess, Persephone sank and rose annually from the underworld, in tune with the natural cycle of sowing and harvesting.

Although usually a faithful husband, Hades at one time became enamoured of the nymph Minthe. When Persephone discovered this, however, she became so jealous that she turned the nymph into the sweet-smelling herb, mint.

HARPIES see *MONSTERS AND FABULOUS BEASTS*

HECATE was believed by some to be descended from the *TITANS*. A Greek goddess with two quite separate aspects, in the day she was supposed to have a benign influence on farming, but during the hours of darkness she was interested in witchcraft, ghosts and tombs. In many ways similar to the vegetation goddess *DEMETER*, Hecate uncomfortably combined fertility with death as a power of the earth. The witch *MEDEA*, *JASON*'s rejected Colchian princess, used to invoke Hecate in her magic arts. Hecate is usually portrayed with three faces. The Athenians were particularly respectful towards her, and once a month they placed offerings of food at crossroads, where her influence was said to be felt.

HECTOR was the eldest son of *PRIAM*, the king of Troy during the Greek siege. The bravest of the Trojan warriors, he was unbeaten on the battlefield. He mistakenly killed Patroclus, the squire and lover of *ACHILLES*, the Greek hero. Achilles had quarrelled with *AGAMEMNON* and refused to fight, but Patroclus borrowed his divine armour in order to rally the Greeks, only to be slain by Hector. Roused from his lethargy, Achilles sought out Hector and compelled him to fight to the death. Such was Achilles' anger that for twelve days he dragged Hector's corpse round Patroclus' tomb. In the end *ZEUS* himself intervened, by sending Achilles' mother *THETIS* to stop this humiliation. So in exchange for a great treasure, Hector's body was returned and properly buried.

43

HELEN was the daughter of *LEDA* and *ZEUS*, the wife of the Spartan king *MENELAUS*, and the cause of the Trojan War. Her immortality as the daughter of the supreme Greek deity suggests that Helen was once a goddess and that her incorporation into myth as an unfaithful queen only occurred when her worship was largely forgotten.

Zeus mated with Leda, wife of the Spartan king Tyndareos, in the guise of a swan. Leda laid an egg, and when Helen hatched from it she brought her up as a member of the royal family. Helen's brothers were Castor and Polydeuces, the mysterious *DIOSCURI*, and her sister was King *AGAMEMNON*'s unfaithful wife *CLYTEMNESTRA*.

At the time of her marriage to Menelaus, the younger brother of Agamemnon, Helen was the most

HELEN (above) paces the walls of Troy. The most beautiful woman of the ancient world, she was also, according to Homer, a thoughtful heroine, given to self-mockery and ever aware of the misery caused by her beauty. (HELEN ON THE WALLS OF TROY BY LORD LEIGHTON, CANVAS, C. 1880.)

desirable bride in Greece. At first Menelaus and Helen were very happy, but then *PARIS*, the eldest son of King *PRIAM* of Troy, visited Sparta and, with the help of the love goddess *APHRODITE*, gained Helen's affection. They even eloped with a part of Menelaus' treasury. When the Trojans refused to return Helen and the stolen treasure, Agamemnon assembled a great army to help his brother Menelaus. For ten years the city of Troy was besieged and then only captured through the trick of the Wooden

Horse. Throughout this long war the sympathies of Helen were mainly with the Greeks, although she was treated as the proper wife, and not merely the mistress, of Paris. After the fall of Troy, Helen and Menelaus were reconciled and they lived undisturbed at Sparta.

HELIOS was the Greek sun god and son of the *TITAN* Hyperion. To the Romans he was known as Sol. It was thought that Helios, after crossing the sky, sailed during the night around the earth in a golden bowl on the encircling waters of *OCEANOS*, and so arrived back in the east just before dawn. Both the Greeks and the Romans held that the inhabited world was a large

HELIOS, god of the sun, appears in works of art as a strong and beautiful youth with gleaming eyes, and a crown of flaming rays. Just as the sun's rays penetrate everywhere, so Helios saw everything, and was invoked as a witness of oaths. (ILLUSTRATION FROM DR SMITH'S CLASSICAL DICTIONARY, 1895.)

island surrounded by an ocean. Although Oceanos was sometimes described as a river, it stretched into the unimaginable distance and far from any shore.

One myth of Helios concerns the death of his son *PHAETHON*. Once this impetuous youth tried to steer his father's radiant chariot, but he quickly lost control. Only the timely action of *ZEUS* steadied its runaway horses and prevented the earth from catching fire. Phaethon fell from the vehicle and was drowned. However, Helios had

many other children, among them Augeas, *CIRCE* and *PASIPHAE*. A gigantic statue of the sun god was erected at the harbour of Rhodes, an island sacred to him. This so-called Colossus was one of the seven wonders of the ancient world, but was toppled by an earthquake around 226 BC.

HEPHAISTOS was the son of *ZEUS* and *HERA*, and was the Greek smith god. His Roman equivalent was *VULCAN*, whose smithy lay beneath the crater of Mount Aetna in Sicily. Hephaistos was lame as a result of having interfered in a quarrel between his parents. So angry did Zeus become that he flung his son from the top of Mount Olympus and let him fall heavily on the volcanic island of Lemnos, in the northern part of the Aegean Sea. In another version, Hera tried to drown her imperfect child, only to be thwarted by sea nymphs who took him to a beach. A sequel to this tale has the smith god gain his revenge as a fully grown man by making a golden throne for his mother which was actually a trap. None of the gods could release Hera, so Hephaistos was invited to return permanently to Mount Olympus. There, under the influence of drink, he was persuaded by his friend *DIONYSUS* to unlock the cunning device and let his mother escape.

Hephaistos seems to have come originally from Asia Minor, where iron mines date from a very early period. His cult was strong in Caria and Lycia, along its south-western shore. His marriage to the love goddess *APHRODITE* may have something to do with this eastern connection, as she also came to Greece from West Asia. Their relationship was almost as tumultuous as that of Zeus and Hera. Once Hephaistos fashioned a trap to catch his unfaithful wife in bed with the war god *ARES*. The Olympian gods merely laughed at Hephaistos' situation; the sea god *POSEIDON* only

HEPHAISTOS, god of fire, fashions exquisite golden works in his fiery forge. Lame, he leans on one leg. By him stands Apollo, who reveals that his wife, Aphrodite, loves Ares, and Hephaistos resolves to trap the guilty pair. (THE FORGE OF VULCAN BY DIEGO VELASQUEZ, CANVAS, 1630.)

promised some remedy if he agreed to release Aphrodite and Ares.

A myth about *ATHENA*'s birth recounts how Hephaistos split open Zeus' head with an axe in order to release the fully grown goddess. Apparently, Zeus had swallowed Athena's mother, Metis, once he realized she was pregnant with a powerful deity. Later, Hephaistos fell in love with Athena, but was rejected by her and his semen fell to earth where it gave birth to the serpent Erichthonius. (See also *FORCES OF NATURE*)

HERA means "lady" and was undoubtedly the title of a powerful mother goddess whom the Greeks inherited from the earlier inhabitants of Argos, which was a major city in the Peloponnese. It was claimed that she was the daughter of *CRONOS* and *RHEA*; however, her addition to the Greek pantheon was not an easy or straightforward matter, as the ceaseless conflicts between her and her husband *ZEUS* readily bear witness. Often her fits of jealousy and quarrelsomeness led to disaster for gods, heroes and men, when she relentlessly persecuted Zeus' mistresses and their children. For example, against the baby *HERACLES*, whom Zeus had fathered in order to help in the coming battle against the *GIANTS*, she sent two serpents to kill him, but the infant hero strangled them

HERA, queen of heaven, directs Helios across the sky. She is crowned with a diadem and veil, symbolizing her status as Zeus' bride. Her sceptre is tipped with a cuckoo, sacred to her as the messenger of spring, the season in which she married Zeus. (ILLUSTRATION FROM STORIES FROM LIVY, 1885.)

in his cradle. However, later in his life, Hera succeeded in driving Heracles temporarily mad.

There are a number of myths about Zeus' courtship of Hera. In one of them he disguised himself as a cuckoo and took shelter inside her clothes during a heavy downpour. Once out of the rain, Zeus resumed his normal shape and promised to marry Hera. Later she bore him the war god *ARES*, the goddess of birth Eileithyia, and Hebe, the cupbearer of the gods. Another child was the smith god *HEPHAISTOS*, who is said in some myths to have been the son of Zeus and Hera, but in others the offspring of Hera alone. Hera was worshipped with particular reverence in Crete and at Samos, where a great temple was said to have been built for her by the *ARGONAUTS*.

HERACLES wrestles with Antaeus, a giant who draws his strength from the earth. To weaken the giant's might, Heracles lifts him high above the earth, and crushes him in mid-air. This bronze expresses the classical ideal of heroic skill and might. (HERCULES AND ANTAEUS BY PIER ANTICO, BRONZE, 1460-1528.)

HERACLES

HERACLES, the son of *ZEUS* and *ALCMENE*, was the greatest of all the Greek heroes. To the Romans he was known as Hercules, and they added various encounters in Italy to his already large cycle of adventures. The name Heracles means "Hera's glory" – a circumstance that firmly ties the hero to Argos, the site of the goddess *HERA*'s temple. It remains a mystery that Heracles should have been persecuted so much by Hera, even going mad at one point during his life.

Because Zeus needed a mortal champion in the forthcoming battle between the gods and the *GIANTS*, he fathered Heracles at the court of Thebes. The chosen mother was Alcmene, the Theban queen. Zeus intended Heracles to be ruler of Mycenae or Tiryns,

HERACLES slays the Hydra, while a crab, sent by the vengeful goddess Hera, nips at his heels. After burning away the Hydra's eight mortal heads, Heracles buried its ninth immortal head under a huge rock in the swamp. (HERCULES AND THE HYDRA, A F GORGUET, CANVAS, C. 1920.)

strongholds close to Argos, but Hera frustrated this plan so well that the hero became the slave of Eurystheus, king of Tiryns. She struck Heracles with a fit of madness, in the course of which he killed his wife and their three sons with arrows. To atone for this terrible deed he had to become Eurystheus' dependent and undertook his famous twelve labours.

These labours began with the killing of the Nemean lion, which could not be harmed by arrows.

Heracles had to fight it with his bare hands and a wooden club. After overcoming the lion, he cured the skin and wore it as a trophy. His next opponent, the Hydra, was a nine-headed serpent sacred to Hera. It lived in a swamp at Lerna, not far from Argos. The problem that the hero encountered when fighting with the Hydra was that for every head he cut off with his sword two new ones grew in its place. But with assistance from his nephew Iolaus he was able to triumph, for Iolaus burned the stumps of the necks as soon as Heracles severed each head. When he returned to Eurystheus, the king refused to count the exploit as a labour, because Heracles had received help from his nephew.

The next labour was not quite so bloody. Heracles had to capture the Ceryneian hind, which was a beast sacred to *ARTEMIS*, goddess of the wild. According to different accounts, he returned to Tiryns with either its golden antlers or the hind itself. Another labour required

him to capture the Erymanthian boar, which plagued the country-side of Arcadia. He trapped it with a net, and during the hunt Heracles encountered a band of *CENTAURS*, beast-like men who lived in woodlands. One of them, Nessus, was later to cause the hero's death.

The fifth labour was the cleansing of Augeas' stables. The son of the sun god, Augeas had vast herds of animals, which he pastured in the kingdom of Elis in the western Peloponnese. King Eurystheus told Heracles to remove the immense piles of dung from the stables, a feat he achieved by diverting the course of a nearby river. The last labour that the hero performed in the Peloponnese was the removal of the Stymphalian birds. Although they had steel-tipped feathers with which they killed both men and animals, these birds were frightened away by the noise of a rattle, which the goddess *ATHENA* had specially made for Heracles.

On the island of Crete the hero tracked down the bull that *MINOS* had failed to sacrifice to the sea god *POSEIDON*. The bull had mated with Minos' wife, *PASIPHAE*, who then gave birth to the *MINOTAUR*, the bull-headed man slain by the Athenian hero *THESEUS*. Heracles captured Poseidon's bull alive and brought it back to Tiryns, where he let it go free at the end of this seventh labour. The eighth labour was more gruesome. It took Heracles to Thrace in pursuit of the man-eating mares of Diomedes, which he subdued after feeding them on their master's flesh.

The last four labours were quite different in nature. First of all Eurystheus had Heracles fetch the girdle of Hippolyta, queen of the fierce *AMAZONS*. Then he captured the cattle of Geryon, a western king who had three heads, three bodies and six hands. After this labour Heracles brought back the golden apples of the *HESPERIDES*, female guardians of the fruit that the earth goddess *GAIA* gave to Hera on her

HERMAPHRODITOS, the beautiful son of Aphrodite and Hermes, inspired the love of the water nymph Salmacis. Here, the golden boy bathes in a shower of sunlight, unaware of his beautiful admirer on the river bank. (SALMACIS AND HERMAPHRODITOS BY BARTHOLOMEUS SPRANGER, CANVAS, C. 1581.)

wedding to Zeus. The last exploit of Heracles was the most testing, for it meant a descent into the underworld, the realm of the dead. From there the hero managed, with some help from *PERSEPHONE*, queen of the underworld, to bring briefly back to Tiryns the three-headed hound *CERBERUS*. As a result of this labour, hard-working Heracles attained immortality for himself. No other hero gained this honour.

Heracles' death on earth, an event that the Greeks expected to precede his translation to Mount Olympus as a god, was the work of the Centaur Nessus, who gave the hero's second wife a poisoned garment for him to wear. Realizing that his death was near, Heracles consulted the Delphic Oracle, which told him to build a funeral pyre in Thessaly. When the dying hero climbed on to it, there was a great flash of lightning and Zeus took his son to join the immortals.

Some of the labours of Heracles are reflected in the names of certain constellations, such as Leo, which represents the Nemean Lion, and Cancer, the crab that was allegedly sent by Hera to help the Hydra. (See also *HEROES*)

HERMAPHRODITOS

was the bisexual offspring of the messenger god *HERMES* and *APHRODITE,* the goddess of love. According to one Greek myth, this handsome boy excited the passion of Salmacis, who was a nymph of a fountain near to the city of Halicarnassus in Asia Minor. When the young Hermaphroditos ignored her attentions, Salmacis prayed to the gods that she might be eternally united with him. The wish was granted when he bathed in some waters and she merged with him physically. The result was a female boy, hence the term hermaphrodite. But Hermaphroditos was not emasculated like Attis, the lover of the Phrygian mother goddess Cybele, for this West Asian god intentionally cut off his own manhood.

HERMES

was the Greek messenger god, and the son of *ZEUS* and Maia. He enjoyed playing tricks and games. During the Trojan War, it was Hermes who was always sent to steal something that was otherwise unobtainable. Before the sea nymph *THETIS* persuaded her son *ACHILLES* to stop mutilating the corpse of *HECTOR*, the gods considered that the simplest solution might be to let Hermes steal the broken body. Hermes was the god who most easily crossed the line between the living and the dead, for the Greeks believed that he guided the dead to the realm of *HADES*, the underworld. This duty helps to explain the later identification of the Germanic god Odin with the Roman equivalent of Hermes, *MERCURY*. Odin was the champion of warriors and the father of the slain.

Hermes is usually depicted as a young man with a wide-brimmed hat and winged sandals, carrying a herald's staff crowned with two snakes. In ancient Greece this staff assured the messenger safe passage even during time of war. Hermes' greatest passion was for the love goddess *APHRODITE*.

The two sons that are attributed to them were both renowned for their unusual sexuality. *HERMAPH-RODITOS* was the first female boy, while the gnome-like Priapus was famous for his enormous penis. Like that of Hermaphroditus, the cult of Priapus originated in Asia Minor, though some distance farther north at Lampascus, near the Black Sea.

HERMES leads Eurydice (centre) and Orpheus (right) through the underworld. As psychopomp, Hermes conducted souls from life on earth to death in Hades. (ILLUSTRATION FROM DICTIONARY OF CLASSICAL ANTIQUITIES, 1891.)

VOYAGERS

THE LURE OF THE UNKNOWN prompts all restless heroes to strike out on a new path in search of a fabulous treasure or shining dream, or for the sheer joy of discovery and adventure. Three intrepid explorers stand out in Classical mythology: Jason, Aeneas and Odysseus. Jason set sail with his fearless crew of Argonauts in search of the Golden Fleece; while Aeneas' seven-year voyage after the fall of Troy led him to the site of future Rome. Most famous and appealing, perhaps, was the fabled Odyssey of the shipwrecked wanderer, Odysseus. Tossed from shore to shore by the angry sea god, Poseidon, he found his way home after ten years' wandering through fabulous lands. The lure of the underworld, or a foray into a monster's den, attracts many heroes, too, such as Theseus who went into the Labyrinth to slay the Minotaur, and found his way out again. Aeneas and Odysseus both journeyed to the underworld in search of prophetic counsel.

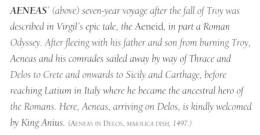

AENEAS' (above) seven-year voyage after the fall of Troy was described in Virgil's epic tale, the Aeneid, in part a Roman Odyssey. After fleeing with his father and son from burning Troy, Aeneas and his comrades sailed away by way of Thrace and Delos to Crete and onwards to Sicily and Carthage, before reaching Latium in Italy where he became the ancestral hero of the Romans. Here, Aeneas, arriving on Delos, is kindly welcomed by King Anius. (AENEAS IN DELOS, MAIOLICA DISH, 1497.)

ORPHEUS (left) went down into Hades, the underworld, to bring back his wife, Eurydice. Charming the shades and even Persephone with his music, he was allowed to take Eurydice back to the upper world as long as he did not look back until clear of Hades. Just as they were about to step out into the light, Orpheus turned round only to see Eurydice slip back into the world of shades forever. Here, Orpheus bids farewell to Eurydice, while Hermes (left), waits to lead Eurydice back through the world of shades. (HERMES, EURYDICE AND ORPHEUS, MARBLE, C. 420 BC.)

ARION (right), a lyrical poet and cithara player, sailed to Sicily to take part in a magical contest which he won. On his way home in a Corinthian ship, he was robbed by the sailors, and forced to leap overboard where he was borne away to safety by song-loving dolphins. Here, Arion plays his cithara on the prow of the ship, invoking the gods of the sea, before leaping overboard. (ILLUSTRATION FROM TANGLEWOOD TALES, C.1920.)

ODYSSEUS (above), celebrated traveller, was renowned for his wits and silver tongue, for his cunning, craft and curiosity. On his way home from Troy, he beached at Sicily, home of the lawless race of one-eyed giants, the Cyclopes. Bold and inquisitive, Odysseus wandered into a Cyclops' den where he and his comrades became trapped by the hostile giant. To escape, they blinded the giant and slipped out, hidden under sheeps' bellies. Here, Odysseus and his comrades pierce the giant's single eye with a sharpened stake. (THE BLINDING OF POLYPHEMUS BY ALESSANDRO ALLORI, FRESCO, 1580.)

JASON (below) sailed across the seas on a perilous voyage in his famous ship, the Argo, accompanied by all the heroes of the age. They went in search of the Golden Fleece, guarded by a watchful dragon at Colchis. After snatching the treasure from under the dragon's eye, Jason and his Argonauts sailed away, finally arriving at Iolcus. Here, Jason steals past with his trophy, casting a furtive glance at a statue of Ares in the sacred grove of the god. (JASON AND THE GOLDEN FLEECE BY ERASMUS QUELLINUS, CANVAS, C. 1670.)

ODYSSEUS (above), fast asleep, is laid on his own coat by Phaeacian sailors. As predicted by the seer, Tiresias, Odysseus reached home alone on a foreign ship, only after many years' wandering. Once back on his island kingdom of Ithaca, he had another battle to fight – with the suitors of his wife – before he could regain his throne and settle down with Penelope. (ILLUSTRATION FROM STORIES FROM HOMER, 1885.)

H

HERO AND LEANDER were one of the great pairs of lovers in Greek mythology. Hero was a priestess of *APHRODITE* at Sestos in the Dardanelles, while Leander lived on the Asian side of the channel at Abydos. They met and fell in love, but because of her religious calling Hero was barred from marriage. In order to keep their affair secret, they arranged that Leander should swim across to Hero each night, guided by a light that she placed in her tower. Next morning he would swim back at dawn. One stormy night the light blew out,

Leander lost his sense of direction and he drowned in the cold waters. When his body was washed ashore at Sestos, Hero threw herself from her tower and died.

THE HESPERIDES were supposedly the daughters of Hesperus, the evening star. Their names were Hespera, Aegle and Erytheis, and they were the guardians of a tree of golden apples given by *GAIA*, mother earth, to the goddess *HERA* on her marriage to *ZEUS*, chief of the Greek gods. This tree stood in the Garden of the Hesperides on the

THE HESPERIDES (right) guarded the golden apples in the garden of the gods. The serpent recalls the myth of the dragon Ladon who guarded the apples until he was slain by Heracles. (THE GARDEN OF THE HESPERIDES BY EDWARD BURNE-JONES, CANVAS, 1869-73.)

HERO (below) looks for her Leander, who usually swam to her across the Hellespont guided by a light in her tower. But her light blew out in a storm and Leander was drowned. (THE LAST WATCH OF HERO BY LORD LEIGHTON, CANVAS, 1880.)

slopes of Mount Atlas in the far west. For one of his labours the hero *HERACLES* tricked the Titan *ATLAS* into getting him the golden apples, offering to hold up the heavens in his stead.

HORATIUS (below), a Roman hero, held the Sublician Bridge, with two of his comrades, against the Etruscan army. While other Romans hacked down the bridge, he held off the enemy until the last moment when he leapt into the stream and swam to safety. (ILLUSTRATION FROM STORIES FROM LIVY, 1885.)

HORATIUS was a Roman hero who saved the early Republic from the Etruscans, when they tried to restore *TARQUINIUS SUPERBUS* to the Roman throne by force of arms. The Etruscans mounted a surprise attack and attempted to capture Rome by crossing a poorly defended bridge over the River Tiber. With two comrades, Horatius held the enemy back until the Romans had destroyed the wooden bridge. As the final supports were sawn away, he ordered his comrades

INO rescues shipwrecked Odysseus by throwing him her veil which saves him from drowning. She was honoured along the Greek shores as a marine deity who aided sailors in distress and guided ships through storms. (ODYSSEUS AND THE GODDESS INO BY ALESSANDRO ALLORI, FRESCO, 1580.)

back to the Roman bank. They just made it, but Horatius was obliged to swim back in full armour. Only prayer saved the hero as he dodged the Etruscan arrows and struggled across the waters of the Tiber.

His full name was Horatius Cocles ("Horatius the one-eyed"). Whether he was wounded in the eye remains uncertain, though tradition says that an ancient statue of a lame, one-eyed man was erected near the bridge in his honour. He was also given as much land as he could drive a plough over in a day. (See also HEROES)

HYPNOS ("Sleep"), in Greek mythology, was the son of Nyx, the night goddess, and the brother of Thanatos ("Death"). Morpheus, the god of dreams, was his son. Hypnos lived in the underworld, the realm of HADES, and never saw the sun. On several occasions HERA asked Hypnos to lull her husband ZEUS to sleep so that she could attack his son HERACLES. Hypnos usually refused to anger Zeus, possibly because he had already come close to having a thunderbolt hurled at him. He was saved by taking refuge with Night, whose power Zeus always respected.

ILUS see FOUNDERS

INO was the daughter of CADMUS, the Phoenician king of Thebes, and Harmonia. In Greek mythology, she brought up DIONYSUS, the son of ZEUS and Semele, who was Ino's dead sister. Semele had been tricked by the goddess HERA, the jealous and vengeful wife of Zeus, who advised her to test the divinity of her lover by telling him to come to her in his true form. This Zeus was also tricked into doing, and the unfortunate result was that he appeared to Semele as lightning and thunderbolts, and she was killed. The unborn Dionysus, however, was taken from her womb and placed in Zeus' own thigh until it was time for his birth. Then, at the suggestion of HERMES, the messenger god, Ino suckled the divine child and kept him safe from Hera. However, such a powerful goddess could not be thwarted without great personal cost. When she discovered the deception, Hera made Ino kill her own children. After she had done this Ino killed herself by jumping off a cliff into the sea. In another myth, she and her infant son Melicertes leapt into the sea and became marine deities.

IO was the daughter of the river god Inachus, and was one of the mortal women who bore children by ZEUS. Although Io was a virgin priestess of HERA, Zeus's wife, at her temple in Argos, this did not prevent Zeus from having her expelled from Argos so that he could make love to her without any difficulties. According to one version, he turned Io into a beautiful heifer, and would have mated with her at once had not Hera guessed his intentions and sent a gadfly to prevent the animal from standing still. It seems that Zeus eventually made love to Io on a cloud over Egypt, where she was returned to her human form. Surprisingly, she was forgiven by Hera. Because Io had been bovine in shape on her arrival, she became identified with the Egyptian cow goddess Hathor.

IO, "the wanderer", was loved by Zeus who changed her into a heifer in order to avoid his jealous wife Hera. Hera ordered all-seeing Argus to watch Io, but Zeus, in his turn, sent Hermes to lull Argus to sleep by the dreamy notes of his flute. (MERCURY AND ARGUS BY PETER PAUL RUBENS, CANVAS, C. 1635.)

IPHIGENIA was the eldest daughter of King *AGAMEMNON* and Queen *CLYTEMNESTRA* of Mycenae. When Agamemnon and the Greek fleet were about to sail for Troy, contrary winds caused by *ARTEMIS* kept the ships at Aulis. The goddess of the forest and wild animals had been offended, either by Agamemnon himself or by an action committed by his father *ATREUS*. In any event, Artemis demanded that Iphigenia should be sacrificed. To bring the sacrificial victim all the way from Mycenae to the port of Aulis in Boeotia, without his wife Clytemnestra's becoming suspicious, Agamemnon pretended that Iphigenia was to be married there to the Greek hero and champion *ACHILLES*. After she discovered his true intention, Clytemnestra never forgave her husband, and years later on his return from the Trojan War helped her lover Aegisthus to murder him.

IXION was a Thessalian king of Larissa and supposedly the son of Phlegyas, though some say his father was *ARES*, god of war. In order to avoid paying a bride-price to Eioneus for his beautiful daughter Dia, Ixion prepared a trap for his unsuspecting father-in-law – a pit filled with fire. Eioneus fell into it on a visit to Larissa and died, and Ixion thus became the first man to shed the blood of a kinsman.

IXION, chained to a rolling wheel, expiates his sins in Tartarus, a hell beneath Hades. Alongside him, fellow prisoners Sisyphus and Tantalus endure their own ordeals – Sisyphus condemned to endless toil and Tantalus to endless thirst. (ILLUSTRATION FROM DR SMITH'S CLASSICAL DICTIONARY, 1895.)

IPHIGENIA, the young daughter of Agamemnon and Clytemnestra, was offered as a "sacrificial lamb" to appease Artemis who was angry with Agamemnon. Here, while the high priest Calchas raises his arms in prayer, Agamemnon (right) bows his head sorrowfully. (ILLUSTRATION FROM STORIES FROM HOMER, 1885.)

Because he was polluted by this unprecedented act, the Thessalian king could not properly rule his land. Perhaps a secret passion for Dia prompted *ZEUS* himself to devise special rites of purification for Ixion. At first Ixion was grateful to the god, but it was not long before he took an interest in *HERA*, Zeus' wife. It was therefore Ixion's turn to be trapped, when Zeus made an exact copy of Hera from a cloud and enticed the unwary king to rape it. The punishment for such sacrilegious crime was to spend eternity in Tartarus, the prison beneath the underworld.

JANUS was a very old Italian god whom the Romans associated with beginnings. In Rome, his double-gated temple in the Forum was always kept open in time of war and closed in time of peace. The month of January – a time for people to look backwards and forwards – was sacred to Janus. There are few myths concerning him, although his extra eyes did on one occasion enable him to catch the nymph Carna, who liked to tease her lovers with sexual advances before suddenly running away. Their son became a king of the important city of Alba Longa.

JASON, the son of Aeson and Philyra, was a Greek hero and voyager, born in Iolcus, a town in Thessalian Magnesia. However, difficulties arose when Aeson, ruler of Iolcus, was deposed by his half-brother Pelias. Either because Philyra distrusted Pelias' intentions towards Jason, or simply because it would better for the boy if he were educated elsewhere, she placed him in the care of the wise Centaur *CHIRON*, who lived in the Thessalian woodlands. Chiron was skilled in many things, including medicine, and may have given the boy the name Jason ("healer").

The Delphic Oracle warned Pelias that he would be turned off the throne of Iolcus by a man wearing only one sandal. So the usurping king was amazed and frightened when a mature Jason arrived

JANUS, a dual-faced god, presided over all that is double-edged in life. His image was found on city gates, which look both inwards and outwards, and he was invoked at the start of each new day and year when people look both backwards and forwards in time. (ILLUSTRATION FROM DR SMITH'S CLASSICAL DICTIONARY, 1895.)

in the city with only one of his sandals. The hero had lost it while carrying what seemed to be an old lady across a swift stream; it was in fact the goddess *HERA* in disguise. Unable to harm the unwelcome guest because he had arrived at the time of a religious festival, Pelias decided to rid himself of the threat he represented by sending Jason on an impossible quest. He offered to name Jason as his successor provided he should bring home from Colchis the Golden Fleece belonging to a wonderful ram which had flown there from Iolcus.

Jason gathered together his companions, who became known as the *ARGONAUTS*, and crossed a sea of marvels, overcame difficult tasks, defeated a guardian serpent and returned with the magic fleece. Part of his success was due to the aid of the Colchian princess and witch, *MEDEA*, whom Jason made his wife with the assistance of the goddess *ATHENA*. On returning to Iolcus, the Argonauts found that Pelias had assumed that they had died in a shipwreck and murdered Jason's father Aeson. Two versions of the myth exist from this point onwards. In one of them Pelias is destroyed by means of Medea's magic. In another the Argonauts, seeing that Pelias will not honour his promise to Jason, sail off to Corinth after failing to capture Iolcus. Jason seems to have accepted exile in Corinth with Medea, where for some ten years they lived happily together and had three sons. Then the hero was offered the hand of a princess named Glauce. When he deserted Medea for her, Jason brought down on his own head the full fury and magical powers of the Colchian princess. For Medea not only killed Glauce but she also destroyed her sons by Jason. Alone and depressed, the hero lingered at Corinth until one day, as he sat in the shade of the *Argo*, his old ship, a piece of rotten timber fell and crushed his skull. (See also *HEROES; VOYAGERS*)

J

JUNO was the Roman equivalent of *HERA*, the wife of *ZEUS*, the chief god of the Greeks. Juno was the queen of the sky and the wife of *JUPITER*. She was always associated with the Greek goddess of birth, Eileithyia, and was called by the Romans "the one who makes the child see the light of day". At the touch of a magical herb specially grown by Flora, the goddess of flowering and blossoming plants, Juno became pregnant with the war god *MARS*. Juno's own warlike aspect is apparent in her attire. She often appears armed and wearing a goatskin cloak, which was the garment favoured by Roman soldiers on campaign. In Rome she was worshipped on the Capitol hill along with Jupiter and *MINERVA*, goddess of wisdom and the arts. The festival of Matronalia was held in her honour on 1 March.

JUNO (below), *the Roman queen of heaven and of womanhood, accompanied every woman through life from birth to death. She is here portrayed in classical style, with a regal diadem, severe hairstyle, and tranquil, majestic air.* (JUNO WITH DIADEM, MARBLE, C. 200 BC.)

L

JUPITER was the Roman sky god, the equivalent of ZEUS. The cult of Jupiter Optimus Maximus ("the best and greatest") began under the Etruscan kings, who were expelled from Rome around 507 BC. At first, Jupiter was associated with the elements, especially storms, thunder and lightning, but he later became the protector of the Roman people and was their powerful ally in war. The games held in the circus in Rome were dedicated to him.

LAIUS, son of Labdacus, king of Thebes, was the father of OEDIPUS and one of the most tragic figures in Greek mythology. The fate that destroyed his family was due to a curse uttered by PELOPS in revenge for Laius carrying off Pelops' young son Chrysippus, who later hanged himself for shame.

In Thebes, Laius took Jocasta as his wife, but they had no children, which the Delphic Oracle told them was fortunate, because Laius was destined to be killed by his own son. For a time Laius and Jocasta did not share the marriage bed. Then one night, full of wine, Laius slept with her and Jocasta conceived a son. So as to overcome the prophecy, the baby was left to die on a distant mountainside, his feet having been cut through with a spike. This action may have been intended to hasten death, but it is not impossible that Laius was also concerned to prevent the child's ghost from walking freely. But the effect was quite the opposite. A shepherd heard the baby's screams and took him to Corinth, where the childless King Polybus adopted him and gave him the name of Oedipus ("swell-foot").

When Oedipus reached manhood he went to Delphi to ask about his parentage. He was told that he would be reunited with his parents in a terrible manner, for he was destined to kill his father and marry his mother. Concluding incorrectly that Corinth was his place of birth, Oedipus travelled towards the north and approached Thebes. On the road he encountered Laius, who was on his way to consult the Delphic Oracle about the SPHINX, a monster with the face and breasts of a woman, the body of a lion and wings, which was causing havoc in the Theban countryside. Oedipus refused to stand aside for the king, a fight ensued and Laius was killed. Thus was Laius' destiny, and the first part of his son's, fulfilled.

LAOCOON was a Trojan, said by some to be the brother of Anchises, and a priest of the sea god POSEIDON. Both the Greeks and the Romans remembered him as the man who warned the Trojans not to accept the so-called Greek gift of the Wooden Horse. He even drove a spear into its side to show his fellow countrymen that inside the hollow belly could lurk a terrible danger to Troy. However, like the prophetess CASSANDRA, Laocoon was ignored. Worse than the fate of Cassandra was that of Laocoon and his two sons, for no Trojan lifted a hand to help when two great sea-serpents suddenly arrived and crushed them to death.

There was no agreement, however, among the Greeks or the Romans about why Laocoon and his sons were killed by the sea-serpents. One opinion was that Laocoon's punishment was not connected with the Trojan War at all. The god of prophecy, APOLLO, was simply punishing the priest for disobeying a divine command. An alternative view was that the death of Laocoon and his sons was the work of ATHENA or Poseidon for causing damage to the dedicatory horse. A Greek named Sinon had informed the Trojans that it was an offering to the goddess Athena: if they destroyed it, then Troy would fall, but if they dragged it inside the city walls, then the Wooden Horse was a guarantee of Troy's safety. In the event the cunning plot worked for the benefit of the Greeks, as those warriors hidden within the horse began a slaughter that led to the eventual overthrow and destruction of the besieged city.

As for the two serpents, once they had crushed Laocoon and his sons to death, they hid themselves in either the temple of Apollo or the temple of Athena.

LAOCOON and his sons were crushed to death by a pair of giant sea-serpents. The ancient poets differed as to the serpents' origin, whether they were sent by Athena or Apollo, and whether Laocoon was innocent or guilty and of what sin. (ILLUSTRATION FROM DICTIONARY OF CLASSICAL ANTIQUITIES, 1891.)

LEDA was loved by Zeus in the shape of a swan. From their union, Leda produced two eggs, one containing the twins, Castor and Polydeuces. As young men, the twins are often depicted with egg-shaped helmets, recalling their unusual parentage. LEDA AFTER LEONARDO DA VINCI, CANVAS, C. 1515-16.)

LETO was the daughter of the *TITANS* Coeus and Phoebe, and she was one of the few Titanesses to be worshipped in ancient Greece. However, her cult was commonly associated with those of her more famous son and daughter *APOLLO* and *ARTEMIS*, whose father was the sky god *ZEUS*. Leto may have given birth to her divine children on the sacred island of Delos, which a helpful *POSEIDON* is said to have fastened permanently to the bottom of the sea with a huge pillar. Later, one of Apollo's most important temples was built on the island. Even the invading Persians respected this sanctuary, when in 490 BC their fleet passed by on its way to punish the Eretrians and Athenians for providing aid to the Greek rebels who were fighting Persia in Asia Minor.

LETO (below), clutching her tiny twins, children of Zeus, flees a giant serpent sent by the vengeful Hera who relentlessly plagued her husband's lovers. The boy, Apollo, plucks a cithara, his attribute as god of the arts, while Artemis clutches a tiny bow, symbol of her role as goddess of the wild. (ILLUSTRATION BY NICK BEALE, 1995.)

LEDA was the daughter of King Thestius of Aetolia, which was a state in north-western Greece. Her husband was King Tyndareos of Sparta. Two of Leda's children were *CLYTEMNESTRA*, the murderous wife of *AGAMEMNON*, and *HELEN*, who was the unfaithful wife of *MENELAUS*, Agamemnon's brother, and the cause of the Trojan War. Leda was also the mother of the *DIOSCURI*, the twin sons Castor and Polydeuces. Various accounts are given of the fathers of her children, for Leda was loved by *ZEUS* who came to her disguised as a swan. Some say that as a result of their union Leda produced two eggs, one contained Clytemnestra and Helen, and the other the Dioscuri, but that Helen's and Polydeuces' father was Zeus while Tyndareos was the father of the mortals Clytemnestra and Castor. In the case of Helen there is little doubt that the myth of the Trojan War turned a goddess into a Queen. She clearly has a connection with older Aegean goddesses who were associated with birds and eggs.

MONSTERS AND FABULOUS BEASTS

CLASSICAL MONSTERS come in all shapes and colours, sometimes hideous, but sometimes bewitchingly fair, sometimes half-human and sometimes entirely demonic. Monsters generally symbolize the dark and unresolved forces in life and in human nature. Greek mythology is full of composite creatures, such as the Chimaera, Sphinx and Scylla, symbolizing complex evil. Not all monsters were cruel, and some, such as Ladon, guarded a precious treasure, while the Sphinx guarded the pass to the city of Thebes. Other monsters ravaged the land, such as the Hydra and Chimaera. Still others were raised by a curse, as when Poseidon sent a sea monster in response to Theseus' rage. Savage beasts, such as satyrs and Centaurs, part human and part animal, represent man's unruly, instinctive nature. Although less awesome than demons, they still harassed and haunted humans.

PYTHON (above), a monstrous serpent, son of Gaia, haunted the caves of Parnassus until slain by Apollo with his first arrows. Apollo founded the Pythian games to commemorate his victory and was afterwards named Apollo Physius. The monster's defeat was celebrated every nine years at the festival of Stepteria at Delphi and involved an enactment of the whole event. (ILLUSTRATION BY GLENN STEWARD, 1995.)

SCYLLA (above), a six-headed sea monster, fished for dolphins, sea-dogs and sailors from her cavern in the Strait of Messina. According to one myth, she was originally a beautiful sea nymph, loved by Zeus and Poseidon in turn, until changed by the jealousy of Circe into a snapping, barking monster. Here, she snatches up the crew of Odysseus as his ship sails past her cavern. (ILLUSTRATION FROM STORIES FROM GREECE AND ROME, 1930.)

THE SIRENS (right) were beautiful sea nymphs who charmed sailors by their alluring songs. Although initially depicted as bird-maids, they later became fair temptresses. Here, Odysseus sails past with his crew; having advised his men to stop their ears with wax, he had himself bound to the mast so that he could hear the sirens' magic song without being lured away. (ODYSSEUS AND THE SIRENS BY FRANCESCO PRIMATICCIO, CANVAS, 1505-70.)

SATYRS (above), wild spirits of the forest, appeared as goat-like creatures with puck noses, bristling hair, budding horns and goat's ears, tails and sometimes hooves. Usually portrayed as wanton and crafty, they frolicked in the forest, chased after nymphs and played impish tricks on men. Here, Diana's forest nymphs are plagued by licentious old satyrs. (DIANA'S NYMPHS CHASED BY SATYRS BY PETER PAUL RUBENS, CANVAS, C. 1670.)

CENTAURS (below), apparently the offspring of Ixion and a cloud, were man-horse beasts who led a wild and savage life in Thessaly, and were fond of riotous revelries. They came to symbolize the dark, unruly forces of nature. The wise Centaur, Chiron, who instructed heroes, was a unique case. Here, the centaurs, writhing in a fierce battle, symbolize the blind and brute force of human nature. (BATTLE OF THE CENTAURS BY ARNOLD BOCKLIN, CANVAS, 1873.)

HARPIES (left), storm goddesses, were feared as robbers and spoilers who raged over battlefields and carried away the weak and wounded or stole children without warning. Originally they were imagined as winged goddesses with beautiful hair. Later on, they appear as awful monsters and spirits of mischief, half-birds, half-maids. (ILLUSTRATION BY GLENN STEWARD, 1995.)

M

LUCRETIA, after her suicide, returned to haunt Sextus Tarquinius, "false Sextus", the high-handed Etruscan who had raped her, incensing the whole of Rome. She appears as a pale, shrouded phantom who sings as she spins through the watches of the night. (ILLUSTRATION FROM LAYS OF ANCIENT

LUCRETIA was the wife of Tarquinius Collatinus and represented the ideal of Roman womanhood. When Sextus, youngest son of the Etruscan king *TARQUINIUS SUPERBUS*, raped her at dagger point around 507 BC, she made her father and her husband promise to avenge her honour before she stabbed herself to death. According to Roman legend, Lucretia's funeral roused the people and their anger was channelled by the inspiring eloquence of Lucius Junius *BRUTUS* into a desire for the overthrow of the monarchy.

MARS, the son of *JUNO* and a magical flower, was originally the Roman god of fertility and vegetation but later became associated with battle. As the god of spring, when his major festivals were held, he presided over agriculture in general. In his warlike aspect he was offered sacrifices before combat and was said to appear on the battlefield accompanied by Bellona, a warrior goddess variously identified as his wife, sister or daughter. Mars, unlike his Greek counterpart,

MARS, god of war, forces himself on gentle Pax and Abundanti, spirits of peace and plenty, while Minerva skilfully steers him away. The allegory dramatizes an age-old conflict, keenly felt in the warring Roman heart. (MINERVA DRIVING MARS BY JACOPO ROBUSTI TINTORETTO, CANVAS, C. 1576.)

ARES, was more widely worshipped than any of the other Roman gods, probably because his sons *REMUS AND ROMULUS* were said to have founded the city.

MEDEA was the daughter of Aietes, king of Colchis, a country adjoining the Black Sea, and the first wife of the voyager *JASON*. Medea means "the cunning one" – a suitable name for a princess skilled in the magic arts. In fact, to the Greeks she hovered somewhere between witch and goddess.

Medea fell in love with the Thessalian hero Jason as soon as he landed in Colchis with the *ARGO-NAUTS*, and she used magic to help him gain the Golden Fleece, the object of their expedition. On the hasty voyage back, when the Colchian fleet gave pursuit, Medea sacrificed her brother to slow the pursuers. On their return to Iolcus, Jason's birthplace, she managed to rejuvenate an old ram by boiling him in a magic pot whereupon he turned into a lamb. She also disposed of Jason's enemy, King Pelias of Iolcus, by persuading his daughters to give him a similar course of beauty treatment, but which killed him. As a result, Jason and Medea were banished to Corinth.

The relations between Jason and Medea went badly wrong. Jason put his first wife aside in order to marry Glauce, a Theban princess. Medea, feeling very insulted, took a terrible revenge on Jason. Glauce was burned alive in a poisoned wedding dress, and Medea saw to it that her own children by Jason were also killed. She then escaped to Athens in a magic chariot, which was said to belong to her grandfather *HELIOS*, the sun god.

In Athens, Medea married its king, *AEGEUS*, and bore him a son named Medus. At this time Aegeus believed he was childless, although he already had a son in the hero *THESEUS*. Through her wily skills, Medea prevailed upon Aegeus to reject Theseus when he came to Athens to claim his inheritance, and she may also have persuaded him to send Theseus to subdue the bull of Marathon. When Theseus succeeded in this dangerous task and at last Aegeus recognized him as his own successor, Medea fled with Medus to Colchis, where they avenged the recent overthrow and death of Aietes. Medus became a ruler of Colchis, but nothing else is known of Medea.

MENELAUS, king of Sparta, was the younger son of *ATREUS*. It was to recover Menelaus' wife *HELEN* that his older brother *AGAMEMNON*, king of Mycenae, led the Greek expedition against Troy. In spite of being warned, Menelaus not only entertained *PARIS*, the eldest son of King *PRIAM* of Troy, but he also

MERCURY (above), as the messenger god of the Romans, was closely identified with the Greek god Hermes. In works of art, he typically wears a winged helmet, or wide-brimmed traveller's hat, and carries a herald's staff, the emblem of peace. (MERCURY AND ARGUS BY PETER PAUL RUBENS, DETAIL, CANVAS, 1635.)

MEDEA, a ruthless sorceress, flees from Colchis with Jason and the Golden Fleece across the seas to Greece, with her father, Aietes, in pursuit. To slow him down, she cut up her brother and cast the parts into the sea, forcing Aietes to pick up the pieces for a pious burial. (THE GOLDEN FLEECE BY H J DRAPER, CANVAS, C. 1880.)

went off to Crete and left Helen alone at Sparta with the handsome visitor. Paris and Helen eloped, taking many of the treasures for which Menelaus was famous.

During the ten-year struggle against Troy, Menelaus played a secondary role to Agamemnon and the other Greek kings, although he was no coward. In single combat with Paris, Menelaus tried to settle the dispute between the Greeks and the Trojans. He won and was only prevented from killing his rival by the intervention of the love goddess *APHRODITE*. She was indebted to Paris for judging her more beautiful than the goddesses *HERA* and *ATHENA*; in gratitude she had given him the love of Helen, the most beautiful woman alive.

After the fall of Troy, Menelaus could not bring himself to kill Helen because of her outstanding beauty. Once again the goddess Aphrodite cast her spell and they were reconciled and returned to Sparta, where they lived happily for many years. When Menelaus died he went to live in the Elysian Fields with his immortal Helen.

MERCURY was the Roman messenger god, and was also the deity who watched over trade and commerce, as his name suggests. He was associated with peace and prosperity. He was apparently imported from Greece around the fifth century BC. Mercury is usually depicted in the same way as his Greek counterpart *HERMES*, with a winged hat and staff.

MIDAS was said to be the son of Gordius and Cybele, or to have been adopted by Gordius. He was the king of Phrygia and renowned for his wealth. According to the Greeks, his fabulous riches were the result of a kindness he showed to *SILENUS*, the old goat-like tutor of *DIONYSUS*, the god of vegetation, wine and ecstasy. So pleased was Dionysus with this behaviour that he offered Midas whatever he wished. The king asked for everything he touched to be turned into gold. At first Midas was overjoyed with the gift, but once he realized that even his food and drink were being transformed on touching his lips, he was horrified. Out of pity

Dionysus told him how to wash away his golden touch, which Midas did in the River Pactolus, thereafter famous for the gold dust to be found on its bed.

Another myth told about Midas concerns a musical competition between the gods *APOLLO* and *PAN*, the divine inventors of the lyre and pipes respectively. When the prize was awarded to Apollo, Midas incautiously expressed his surprise at the outcome and received from Apollo a set of ass's ears for his foolish presumption.

MIDAS, the fabled king of Phrygia, was fabulously rich, yet chose, when granted a wish by the gods, to become richer still, by asking for everything he touched to turn to gold. His wish was granted, but joy quickly turned to grief when he could neither eat nor drink. (ILLUSTRATION BY NICK BEALE, 1995.)

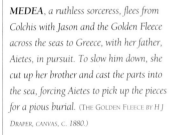

MENELAUS (left) was usually a gentle, even-tempered man, but here he fights firercely over the fallen body of Patroclus who lies naked, for Apollo had struck off his helmet, splintered his ash spear and broken his corselet, stripping him bare so that he would be easily killed by Hector. (ILLUSTRATION FROM STORIES FROM HOMER, 1885.)

N

MINERVA (whose name may have originally meant "thought") was the Roman goddess of wisdom and the arts, the equivalent of the Greek goddess ATHENA. She was worshipped throughout Italy, though only in Rome did she take on a warlike character. Minerva is usually depicted wearing a coat of mail and a helmet, and carrying a spear. The Romans dedicated the spoils of war to her.

MINOS was the son of ZEUS and EUROPA and became the king of Crete, with his palace situated at Knossos. The Greeks regarded him both as a just lawgiver and as a cruel oppressor. To build his wonderful palace, Minos employed the Athenian craftsman DAEDALUS, whose creations were thought to be almost divine. So lifelike were his statues, for instance, that they had to be chained down in order to stop them running away. Minos was less pleased, however, with the hollow cow that Daedalus made for his queen, PASIPHAE, so that she might satisfy her desire for the white bull which POSEIDON had sent from the waves as a sign that Minos should ascend the Cretan throne. The MINOTAUR, a man with a bull's head, was the outcome of Pasiphae's unnatural union. This monstrous creature was housed in the Labyrinth, a special maze built by Daedalus at Minos' request.

Minos was known to the Greeks as an ancient ruler of the seas. His naval strength could well have owed something to Daedalus' inventiveness. Certainly he was not prepared for another ruler to enjoy the remarkable services of the craftsman. When Daedalus and his son Icarus left Crete without permission, Minos sailed to Sicily in hot pursuit. There, in the city of Kamikos, Minos met his death. Daedalus had arrived in Sicily as a refugee. He quickly went to ground and was hidden by King Cocalos of Kamikos. In order to find out where the craftsman was hiding,

MINERVA (above), the Roman goddess of wisdom, is depicted here taming a wild Centaur, who symbolizes the dark unruly side of human nature. His yearning expression suggests man's longing for divinity, despite himself. (MINERVA AND THE CENTAUR BY SANDRO BOTTICELLI, CANVAS, C. 1482.)

Minos carried a shell and promised to reward anyone who could pass a thread through it. Daedalus alone could solve the problem, which eventually he was unable to resist. When King Cocalos, on Daedalus' behalf, claimed the prize, Minos demanded that the craftsman be surrendered to him. But the daughters of Cocalos were unwilling to lose the inventive man who made them beautiful toys, and with his help they plotted Minos' death. When they took their royal guest to the bathroom, Daedalus led a pipe through the roof and boiling water, or oil, was poured down upon the

THE MINOTAUR (below) wrestles with Theseus in the Labyrinth, which is represented by the meander pattern at the sides. The bull-baiters above illustrate the sport of bull-leaping, part of the mysterious bull-cult of ancient Crete. (THE BULL-BAITERS BY JOHN DUNCAN, WATERCOLOUR, C. 1880.)

unsuspecting Cretan king. After his death Minos became a stern judge in the realm of HADES, the underworld, the land of the dead.

THE MINOTAUR was the monstrous son of a white bull, which was sent by the sea god POSEIDON, and PASIPHAE, the wife of King MINOS of Crete. When the child was born it had the head of a bull and the body of a man, and was given the name Minotaur ("Minos' bull").

The creature was fed on seven boys and seven girls sent annually as tribute by the Athenians. To free his countrymen of this terrible burden the hero THESEUS came to Knossos, entered the maze-like Labyrinth where the Minotaur lived and killed it. He was assisted by King Minos' daughter ARIADNE, who gave him a ball of thread, instructing him to unravel it on his way into the maze so that he could find his way out again. She also gave Theseus a sword.

In the strange story of the Minotaur the Greeks recalled in a garbled form the glories of the older inhabitants of Crete. It is now known that the bull games of the ancient Cretans involved young athletes leaping over bulls, even attempting somersaults holding the horns. Although some of them doubtless sustained serious injury, or may even have been killed, there is nothing to suggest that a man-eating creature was involved.

MOERAE see FATES

THE MUSES, from the Roman name, Musae, were the daughters of ZEUS and Mnemosyne, a TITAN, whose name means "memory". They used to dance and sing at parties held by the gods and heroes. For the Greeks, the Muses were the inspiration of poetry, music and dance. Later, other intellectual activities were added to their care. Although accounts of their number differ, it is generally accepted that

the echo of her voice. Narcissus was then condemned by Nemesis, goddess of retribution, to spend the rest of his days admiring his own reflection in a pool. At last he died and was turned into the flower that bears his name.

NEPTUNE was an ancient Italian water god whom the Romans identified with *POSEIDON*. Compared to Poseidon, however, Neptune plays a minor role in Roman mythology.

NOTUS see *FORCES OF NATURE*

OCEANOS was a *TITAN*, the son of Ouranos and *GAIA*, but never an enemy of *ZEUS*. On the contrary, he protected Zeus' wife *HERA* and mother *RHEA* when the gods fought the Titans. As ruler of the encircling sea, which the Greeks believed surrounded the world, Oceanos married his sister Tethys and they produced three thousand rivers.

THE MUSES, guiding spirits of the arts, inspired all gifted artists, though they resented any serious competition and deprived the Sirens of their feathers for daring to be better than them in song. The nine Muses appear here amid the aspiring artists of the Renaissance. (THE REALM OF THE MUSES BY LORENZO COSTA, CANVAS, C. 1506)

there were nine Muses altogether – Clio, Euterpe, Thalia, Melpomene, Terpsichore, Erato, Polyhymnia, Urania and Calliope.

NAIADS see *FORCES OF NATURE*

NARCISSUS, according to Greek mythology, was the beautiful son of the River Cephissus in Boeotia and the nymph Liriope. Among the many who loved him, including immortals and mortals, was Echo, who slowly pined away, leaving just

NARCISSUS (right), a beautiful youth, was loved by the nymph Echo who, failing to attract him, died of grief. He, in his turn, fell in love with his own reflection and pined away until changed by the gods into the flower that bears his name. (ECHO AND NARCISSUS BY J W WATERHOUSE, CANVAS, 1880.)

OCEANUS (left), father of the river gods, is depicted here with a typically tempestuous face, unruly locks and horned brow. Above him, Selene, the crescent moon, sheds a mild light; and on either side flash the stars, Phosphorus (left) and Hesperus (right). (ILLUSTRATION FROM DICTIONARY OF CLASSICAL ANTIQUITIES, 1891.)

61

ODYSSEUS *alights on the island of Aeaea where he is warned by Hermes of the horrors of Circe's enchanting wine, which turns men into swine. This fate has already befallen one comrade and so Odysseus must keep his guard.* (CIRCE WITH THE COMRADES OF ODYSSEUS BY ALESSANDRO ALLORI, FRESCO, 1580.)

ODYSSEUS, king of Ithaca, was one of the Greek leaders who took part in the Trojan War. He was celebrated for both his part in this conflict and his remarkable voyage home to his island kingdom in the Ionian Sea.

A brave and clever man, Odysseus was sometimes thought to have been the son of *SISYPHUS,* the trickster of Greek mythology. But his real father was probably Laertes, whom he succeeded as king of Ithaca. His mother was named Anticleia and his faithful wife Penelope was the sister of King Tyndareos of Sparta.

From the start of the campaign against Troy it is clear that King *AGAMEMNON,* the Greek leader, placed great store upon Odysseus' cunning. He was sent with Nestor, the aged king of Pylos, to discover where the great warrior *ACHILLES* was hidden. Again, at Aulis, where the Greek fleet was stranded by contrary winds, it was Odysseus who tricked Agamemnon's wife *CLYTEMNESTRA* into sending her daughter *IPHIGENIA* from Mycenae, supposedly to marry Achilles. Instead, however, Iphigenia was to be sacrificed to *ARTEMIS,* goddess of the wild, in order to obtain a fair wind to Troy. Throughout the ten-year struggle against the Trojans, Odysseus was important not so much as a fighter but as a counsellor and a schemer. His eloquence was renowned, and it was probably Odysseus who thought of the Wooden Horse, which gave the Greeks victory.

Odysseus deceived the Trojans with this horse built of wood whose hollow belly was filled with Greek warriors under his own command. The Trojans dragged the Wooden Horse inside their walls when they learned from a Greek, deliberately left behind when the rest put to sea, that the offering would bring their city a guarantee of divine protection. But during the night the Greeks emerged from it, and surprised the Trojans. Hence, the ancient saying "Never trust the Greeks bearing gifts".

Although Troy fell, the wildness of the looting and the slaughter deeply offended the gods. In particular, the goddess *ATHENA* was enraged at the rape of *CASSANDRA* within the sanctuary of her own temple. Odysseus tried to appease Athena, and he escaped drowning in the great storm which the angry goddess sent to shatter the victorious Greek fleet on its homeward journey. But he could not entirely avoid blame, and *POSEIDON* saw to it that he was the last Greek leader to reach home, after a voyage lasting some ten years.

The long period of wandering that Odysseus suffered was a favourite story of both the Greeks and the Romans, who knew the voyager by the name of Ulysses. The exact route that he followed remains a mystery, not least because his travels took him beyond known territory and into strange and dangerous lands. From Troy Odysseus sailed first to

ODYSSEUS *raises his great bow and, with effortless might, stretches the bowstring which the suitors had struggled in vain to bend. He then slays the suitors who have devoured his wealth and plagued his wife during his long voyage home.* (ILLUSTRATION FROM STORIES FROM HOMER, 1885.)

Thrace, where he lost many of his men in battle. After this bloody incident the places he touched upon are less easy to identify. Storms drove him to the land of the Lotophagi ("the lotus-eaters"), whose diet made visitors forget their homelands and wish to stay on forever. Then he encountered in Sicily, it was later believed, the Cyclops *POLYPHEMUS*, whose father was Poseidon. By putting out Polyphemus' single eye when the gigantic man was befuddled with wine, Odysseus and his companions managed to escape becoming his dinner. They then arrived on the floating island of Aeolus, who was the ruler of the winds. There Odysseus received a rare present, a sack full of winds. The idea appears in many different mythologies, but according to the Greeks, it was of little use on the voyage because the curiosity of Odysseus' men got the better of them and they opened the sack and the winds no longer blew in a helpful direction.

A tragedy overcame the squadron of ships that Odysseus led among the Laestrygones, a race of giant cannibals. Only his own ship survived the attack and reached Aeaea, the island of the enchantress *CIRCE*, later considered to be situated off Italy. Odysseus resisted her spells, with the aid of the messenger god *HERMES*, and made the enchantress restore to human shape his men who had been turned to swine. Afterwards, on Circe's advice, he sailed to the western edge of the encircling sea, the realm of *OCEANOS*, where ghosts came from the underworld realm of *HADES* to meet him. The shade of the blind seer *TIRESIAS* gave Odysseus a special warning about his homeward journey to Ithaca. He told him that if the cattle of the sun god *HELIOS* on the isle of Thrinacia were harmed by him he would never reach his home. The ghost of Odysseus' mother also spoke of the difficulties being faced by Penelope in Ithaca at the time. The ghost of Agamemnon, his old comrade-in-arms, also warned him about his homecoming; when he returned home he had been murdered by his wife and lover in the bathroom.

Turning eastwards, Odysseus sailed back towards Greece and was the only man who dared to listen to the alluring song of the Sirens, bird-women of storm. He filled his men's ears with wax and had himself bound with strong cords to the mast. Odysseus then passed through the straits between Sicily and Italy, where six of his crew were seized by the six-headed monster Scylla. On the island of Thrinacia, as Tiresias had foretold, the voyagers were tempted by hunger to slay some of Helios' cattle. Despite his warning, the desperate men killed and cooked several cows when Odysseus was asleep. Later they deserted him, but were drowned in a storm sent by *ZEUS* at Helios' request.

Alone, Odysseus was almost swallowed by the great whirlpool Charybdis. In an exhausted state he drifted to the wondrous island of the sea nymph Calypso, who cared for him and eventually proposed marriage. But not even immortality would tempt him, and after seven years the gods forced Calypso to let Odysseus set off again. Shipwrecked once more in the land of the Phaeacians, he was welcomed as an honoured guest and offered a passage back to Ithaca. So it was that he was secretly landed near his own palace, which he entered disguised with Athena's aid as a beggar.

Penelope had been patiently awaiting Odysseus' return from the war. Although pressed to marry one of her many noble suitors, she had put them off for a while by pretending that she could not marry until she had finished weaving a shroud for Laertes, her father-in-law. But Penelope unravelled it each night, until one of her maids betrayed the trick. Finally, after ten years, Penelope agreed to marry the suitor who could bend and string Odysseus' great bow. This challenge was proposed on the advice of the goddess Athena. The only suitor who succeeded at the challenge was a beggar, who then threw off his disguise and revealed himself as Odysseus.

Assisted by his son Telemachus and two loyal retainers, Odysseus dispatched the suitors and hanged the treacherous maids. Reunited with his family at last, including his father Laertes, Odysseus then defeated an attack by the relations of the suitors and returned Ithaca to peace. Zeus himself threw down a thunderbolt to signal an end to the fighting. (See also *VOYAGERS*)

OEDIPUS ("swell-foot") was the unlucky son of King *LAIUS* and Queen Jocasta of Thebes. Because, as a guest at the court of *PELOPS*, Laius had taken sexual advantage of Pelops' young son Chrysippus, a curse was laid on the ruling house of Thebes. Indeed, an oracle warned Laius that any son Jocasta bore him would kill him. For a long time the king and queen abandoned the marriage bed, but drink one night caused Laius to throw caution to the winds and a son was duly conceived. At birth, the infant was pierced in the feet and left to die on a distant mountainside, a fairly common practice for unwanted children in ancient Greece. However, a shepherd found the baby and took it to King Polybus of Corinth, who, having no children, adopted the boy and chose the name of Oedipus because of his damaged feet. When he grew up, Oedipus was taunted that he was not Polybus' son, so he went to ask

OEDIPUS, after years of wandering since his exile from Thebes, leans on his loyal daughter Antigone; they travel to Colonus where it is destined that Oedipus will finally find peace and death in a sacred grove.

(ILLUSTRATION BY NICK BEALE, 1995.)

the Delphic Oracle about his parentage. He was told that he was destined to kill his father and marry his mother, and in horror he fled north. *En route* he encountered Laius, whose charioteer deliberately ran over Oedipus' foot. The result was that Oedipus killed everyone there, except one of his father's servants who ran away.

Arriving in Thebes, Oedipus discovered its people were greatly distressed at the news of Laius' death and terrified of the *SPHINX*, an ugly monster causing havoc in the countryside. When the regent *CREON* announced that whoever rid the city of the Sphinx would be offered the throne and the hand of

ORESTES (right) finds some peace at the shrine of Apollo in Delphi where he has fled, pursued by the Furies, after murdering his mother. At Delphi, Orestes is partly purified by Apollo, and even the Furiae, asleep on the altar, find rest. In time, Orestes is acquitted by the Areopagus.

(ORESTES, MARBLE, C. 200 BC.)

OEDIPUS puzzles over the Sphinx's riddle, which she challenges all travellers to Thebes to solve. When Oedipus outwits the Sphinx, she flings herself into the chasm below and destroys herself. Oedipus is portrayed here, as he is in ancient art, as a calm and pensive hero. (OEDIPUS AND THE SPHINX BY JEAN AUGUSTE INGRES, CANVAS, 1808.)

Jocasta, Oedipus decided to try or die in the attempt. By outwitting the Sphinx and causing its death, Oedipus unwittingly fulfilled his own destiny: he had killed his father, now he married his mother.

For a time Oedipus and Jocasta lived happily together, having a family of two sons, Polynices and Eteocles, and two daughters, *ANTIGONE* and Ismene. Then a dreadful plague settled on Thebes, and Creon was sent to ask the Oracle at Delphi for a remedy. The divine command he brought back to the city was to drive out the murderer of Laius. Although the famous seer *TIRESIAS* announced

that Oedipus was the guilty one, the new king would not believe this was true until he traced those involved in his own exposure as a child. Convinced at last of his exceptional crime, Oedipus blinded himself and left Thebes. His mother and wife, Jocasta, had already committed suicide. In the company of his daughter Antigone, a broken Oedipus eventually found spiritual peace in a sacred grove at Colonus near Athens. His death there was considered to be a good omen by the Athenians, because in gratitude for the sanctuary he was given, Oedipus had foretold that his bones would save them from any future attack by the Thebans.

ORESTES was the son of King *AGAMEMNON* of Mycenae and *CLYTEMNESTRA* and is renowned for having committed matricide. In ancient Greece there were many places associated with his purification after such a terrible crime. For example, in front of the sanctuary of *APOLLO* in Troezen, there was a hut used by Orestes, which was said to have been built to avoid receiving the polluted murderer as a guest in a normal house.

When Agamemnon left to lead the Greek expedition against Troy, his wife Clytemnestra took a lover, Aegisthus. When Agamemnon returned, some ten years later, the two lovers murdered him, and it was to avenge this crime that Orestes killed his mother. The great horror felt by the Greeks over Orestes' actions runs deep in his myth. Correct though he was to seek vengeance for his father's murder, as the Delphic Oracle had advised him to, the killing of a mother by her son could not be expected to bring anything other than dire misfortune. The *FURIES* were avenging deities who tracked down all those with blood on their hands, and they now relentlessly pursued Orestes.

Wild-eyed and distraught, Orestes wandered as an outcast

throughout Greece. When finally he went to Delphi for help, since Apollo had advised him to slay his father's murderers, Orestes was told to go to Athens and stand trial by the Areopagus, an ancient council presided over by *ATHENA*. The verdict in his favour calmed the Furies, so they were renamed the Eumenides ("the soothed goddesses"). It is likely, however, that the Greeks called them by this euphemism because they were afraid to use their real name, the Erinyes, "the angry ones"

ORION see *GIANTS*

ORPHEUS was a Thracian singer much revered in ancient Greece. He was said to be the son of Calliope, *MUSE* of epic poetry. His chief myth concerns the death of his wife, the nymph Eurydice. One

day she died of a snake bite. Orpheus was so saddened and grief-stricken by this sudden loss that he no longer sang or played. Then he decided to risk his own life in a desperate journey to the land of the dead in the forlorn hope of bringing Eurydice home. By using his miraculous music, Orpheus was able to charm the boatman, Charon, who ferried him across the Styx, and the three-headed *CERBERUS* so that he could enter the underworld. Even the ghosts of the dead were greatly moved by his song, but the rulers of the underworld, *HADES* and his wife *PERSEPHONE*, granted Orpheus his only desire on one condition: under no circumstances was Orpheus to look back at Eurydice until both of them were completely returned to the land of the living. But so overcome was the singer by love for his

ORPHEUS, after his death, became an oracle, and is pictured here being consulted by a Thracian maid. His head rests on a lyre that is encrusted with seaweed because, ever musical, even in death his decapitated head had floated downstream calling for Eurydice. (A THRACIAN MAID WITH THE HEAD OF ORPHEUS BY GUSTAVE MOREAU, CANVAS, 1865.)

departed wife that just before they reached the surface of the ground, he could not resist a quick glance in the half-light. The result was that Eurydice turned into a ghost again and sank back to Hades' kingdom forever. Orpheus' own fate was to be dismembered by Thracian maenads, the female worshippers of *DIONYSUS*, the god of vegetation, wine and ecstasy. Apparently, they tore the singer to pieces except for his head, which was then cast into a river and went floating downstream calling out "Eurydice!"

Ancient fascination with this romantic story was probably connected with religious ceremonies and rituals that were aimed at securing personal salvation after death. The worshippers of both Orpheus and Dionysus believed in some form of afterlife. Paintings of Orpheus have even been found in the catacombs, the early burial chambers of Christians in Italy. (See also *VOYAGERS*)

ORPHEUS was pursued and torn apart by the frenzied maenads, who were the wild devotees of Dionysus. They were usually depicted, as they are here, whirling in ecstasy, with swirling robes, and dishevelled, snakebound hair. (ILLUSTRATION FROM DR SMITH'S CLASSICAL DICTIONARY, 1895.)

FORCES OF NATURE

THE WONDERS AND MYSTERIES OF NATURE are explained in mythology through the will and actions of the gods. Sunrise and sunset, storms and tidal waves, summer and winter unfold as part of a divine drama. For the ancient Greeks, the sun rose and set because Phoebus Apollo drove the glittering sun-chariot on a fiery course across the sky, preceded by Eos who sprinkled morning dew from her vase. Springtime came when Persephone, who symbolized the seed-corn, rose from the underworld to live in the light of day with her mother, Demeter, goddess of corn. The tempestuous sea god, Poseidon, could stir up sea-storms, or soothe the waves; while mighty Zeus could strike from afar with a bolt of lightning or brighten the sky with rainbows. In addition to the great gods of sky, land and sea, nature spirits or nymphs infused the forests, fields and rivers.

APOLLO (above), god of light, symbolized not only sunlight – for originally Helios (the sun) radiated daylight and was only later identified with Apollo – but also the bright, life-giving, pure, healing light of divinity. Apollo's light underlies his other roles as god of healing, god of prophecy and god of the arts. He withdrew in winter to sunny Lycius and returned in spring to dispel winter. Here, he drives the sun-chariot on its course across the heavens. (ILLUSTRATION FROM STORIES FROM LIVY, 1885.)

POSEIDON (above), the turbulent god of the seas, symbolized the might of the sea-storm. He dwelt in a golden palace in the depths of the ocean, and rode the waves in his sea-chariot, drawn by sea-horses, speeding so fast that he passed from Samothrace to Aegae in three great strides. Beside him basks his wife, the sea nymph Amphitrite, while a school of tritons (part men, part fish) frisk around his chariot blowing their conches, which they used to raise or calm the waves. (POSEIDON AND HIS CHARIOT BY MIRABELLO CAVALORI, C. 1497.)

ZEUS (left), the chief deity, governed the winds and clouds, rain, thunder and lightning. By striking his aegis he caused storms and tempests to rage, but equally, he could calm the elements and brighten the sky. As the father of the hours, he governed the changing seasons. An awesome but benign god, he is seen here resplendent in fiery light, bearing his aegis, symbol of his sovereign power over all forces of nature and all other gods. (JUPITER AND SEMELE BY GUSTAVE MOREAU, CANVAS, DETAIL, 1896.)

FLORA (right), blooming Roman goddess of spring, was honoured every year at the time of the Floralia, a theatrical festival when the people decked themselves in flowers and enjoyed a great feast lasting for six days. Flora, serene and benign, is here honoured in a lavish parade. Poussin's atmospheric scene vividly revives the pagan splendour of the early Greek pastoral festivals. (THE TRIUMPH OF FLORA BY NICOLAS POUSSIN, CANVAS, C. 1627.)

HEPHAISTOS (below), the smith god, is typically depicted as a grave, intense man wearing a workman's cap and immersed in his fiery craft. He had forges beneath volcanoes but also on Olympus where 20 bellows worked at his bidding. Famed for his artistry, he crafted works of wonder, such as Achilles' shield, embossed with a dramatic scene of life and death, joy and grief, peace and war. (APOLLO IN THE FORGE OF HEPHAISTOS BY DIEGO VELASQUEZ, CANVAS, DETAIL, 1630.)

THE NAIADS (above), or water nymphs, dwelt beside running water. Like their cousins, the Nereids and Oceanids of the oceans, the Oreads of the hills and the Dryads of forests and trees, they were usually sweet, benign spirits. Naiads, especially, were helpful and healing, nurturing fruits, flowers and mortals. Yet the youth Hylas who went to draw water from a pool was lured by the nymphs into the water and never seen again. (HYLAS AND THE WATER NYMPHS BY J W WATERHOUSE, CANVAS, C. 1890.)

NOTUS (below), the south wind, brought with it fog and rain. Here, as a winged deity, Notus pours rain from a vase, much as his mother, Eos, goddess of dawn, sprinkles dew from a vase before the sun-chariot in the early morning. (ILLUSTRATION FROM DR SMITH'S CLASSICAL DICTIONARY, 1891.)

ZEPHYRUS (below), the west wind, dwelt with his brother wind, Boreas, in a palace in Thrace. He was father of the immortal horses, Xanthus and Balius, Achilles' battle steeds who galloped with the speed of wind. (ILLUSTRATION FROM DR SMITH'S CLASSICAL DICTIONARY, 1891.)

P

PAN (above) plays his pipes at dusk. As a spirit of the dark forest, he often startled solitary travellers, arousing sudden awe and panic. He is usually depicted with shaggy head, goat's horns and hooves, dancing or playing a syrinx. (ILLUSTRATION FROM TANGLEWOOD TALES, C. 1920.)

PAN was the son of the messenger god *HERMES*. As the Greek god of the mountainside, the pastures of sheep and goats, he was himself goat-horned and goat-legged. Pan was especially associated with Arcadia, the mountainous state in central Peloponnese. He was playful and energetic, but very irritable, especially if disturbed during his afternoon nap. He liked to play on a pipe, which was known as a syrinx after a nymph of that name who turned herself into a reed-bed to avoid his advances. For Pan could also be a frightening god when he blew on his conch. Our

PANDORA (below), "all-gifts", was the first woman to appear on earth, created by the gods to work mischief for men. Irrepressibly curious, she could not resist opening a sealed jar, containing the horrors of life: strife and sickness, sorrow and grief. (ILLUSTRATION BY NICK BEALE, 1995.)

word "panic" derives from this aspect of his divinity. His worship spread from Arcadia to Athens immediately after the Athenian and Plataean victory over the Persians at Marathon in 480 BC, because he made the Persians flee in panic. He rendered a similar service for *ZEUS* during the battle against *CRONOS* and the *TITANS*. His conch deeply worried Zeus' opponents.

PANDORA was the Greek Eve, the bringer of all sorrows for mankind. She was the first woman and was created by *HEPHAISTOS*, the smith god, on *ZEUS'* orders in

order to upset *PROMETHEUS*, the Greek god of fire and friend of men. When she went to live among men, she was given a gift from the gods which was a sealed jar that contained all the misfortunes of existence. But soon Pandora's great curiosity overcame a natural fear of what might be inside, and she broke the seal, releasing sorrow, disease and conflict. As a result, the men who originally comprised the human race gained a mortal, female companion, but also untold woes. Appropriately, the name Pandora means "all gifts" – the bad as well as the good.

PARIS (above), the judge of a divine beauty contest, chose Aphrodite as the winner because she offered him the world's fairest woman. Behind her, wise Athena had promised him fame, while queenly Hera had offered him power. (THE JUDGEMENT OF PARIS BY JEAN REGNAULT, CANVAS, 1820.)

PARIS was one of the fifty sons of King *PRIAM* of Troy. According to the Greeks, he was responsible for causing the Trojan War. Paris was a very handsome young man and wooed *HELEN* so well that she left her husband *MENELAUS*, king of Sparta, and fled with her lover to Troy. His unusual attractiveness was believed to have been a gift from *APHRODITE*, the goddess of love. In return for choosing her as the fairest of goddesses, Aphrodite offered Paris the most beautiful woman in the world, Helen.

During the long siege of Troy Paris cut a poor figure as a warrior. His single combat with Menelaus, Helen's husband, was supposed to have settled the outcome of the whole war. Instead it revealed Paris as a coward, who only escaped with his life through the intervention of Aphrodite. As a result, the Trojan champion *HECTOR*, his eldest brother, treated him very badly. It was an irony of fate that a poisoned arrow shot from Paris' bow should have found the one vulnerable spot on the mighty Greek champion *ACHILLES*, his heel. Paris himself was killed by an arrow, prior to the fall of Troy.

PASIPHAE

PASIPHAE, in Greek mythology, was the daughter of *HELIOS*, the sun god, and wife of *MINOS*, king of Crete. The sea god *POSEIDON* sent a white bull as a sign of Minos' right to rule the island, but the king refused to sacrifice the animal when it emerged from the waves, and Poseidon pronounced a curse in anger at the lack of respect

PEGASUS, a magnificent winged horse, dips and dives through the flames of the fire-breathing monster, the Chimaera. On his back, Bellerophon urges him on. The hero had successfully tamed Pegasus with a golden bridle given to him by Athena.
(ILLUSTRATION FROM TANGLEWOOD TALES, C. 1920.)

shown to himself. Pasiphae was to be stricken with a passionate desire for the bull. In order to gratify her lust, the great craftsman *DAEDALUS* made a cow, into which Pasiphae fitted and so could mate with the bull. Later, she gave birth to the *MINOTAUR* ("Minos' Bull"), which was kept in the Labyrinth.

PEGASUS

PEGASUS, in Greek mythology, was the flying horse belonging to the Corinthian hero *BELLEROPHON*. The winged steed was born from blood which spilled from the severed head of the *GORGON* Medusa, who was already pregnant by the sea god *POSEIDON* (a deity always associated with bulls and horses). Bellerophon was given a magic bridle by *ATHENA* to help him tame Pegasus. When the hero tried to fly to Mount Olympus, Pegasus threw him on the instruction of *ZEUS*.

PELOPS

PELOPS was the son of King *TANTALUS*, the ruler of a kingdom in Asia Minor. Pelops' name is still recalled in the Peloponnese ("the isle of Pelops"), which is the large peninsula of southern Greece.

PASIPHAE, queen of Crete, was drawn irresistibly to a mysterious white bull which emerged from the waves. She developed a strange passion for the bull, and from her union with the creature she bore a dreadful bull-man, the Minotaur, who was kept hidden in an underground maze.
(ILLUSTRATION BY NICK BEALE, 1995.)

The sea god *POSEIDON* so loved Pelops that he seized the youth and carried him off to Mount Olympus. Possibly because of this divine favour shown to his son, Tantalus was honoured by the gods as no other mortal. He was allowed to eat nectar and ambrosia, the immortal food served to the deities on their mountain home. But Tantalus fell from divine favour and suffered eternal torment as a result.

According to one version of the myth, Tantalus cut up, boiled and served his own son Pelops to the gods in order to test their omniscience. Only *DEMETER*, the goddess of vegetation, partook of the feast, inadvertently eating a piece of Pelops' shoulder. Later, when the gods returned the youth to life, the missing piece of his body was replaced by ivory.

By favour of Poseidon the restored Pelops became famous as a champion charioteer, which was an accomplishment that the ancient Greeks regarded as one of the greatest. So when Oenomaus, king of Elis, offered his daughter Hippodameia in marriage and also his lands to anyone who could defeat him in a chariot race, Pelops accepted the challenge. But he had to agree that Oenomaus could shoot an arrow at him if he caught up with his chariot. Thirteen contestants had already perished.

It was said that Pelops bribed a certain Myrtilus, the king's charioteer, to remove the linchpins from his master's chariot, but when he won Pelops refused to acknowledge this assistance. In different versions of the story, he either threw Myrtilus into the sea, or he spurned him. As a consequence, the father of Myrtilus, who was the messenger god *HERMES*, saw that a curse afflicted the descendants of Pelops. The consequences of this curse on the house of *ATREUS*, Pelops' eldest son and the father of *AGAMEMNON*, is the basis for that family's tragic story.

PELOPS, in the winning chariot, races along the Greek track, fast outstripping his rival Oenomaus, whose chariot swerves and crashes. Pelops' white shoulder was made of ivory, fashioned by the gods after he had been partly eaten by Demeter. (ILLUSTRATION BY GLENN STEWARD, 1995.)

PENELOPE was the daughter of Icarius, king of Sparta, and a nymph Peribaea. As the faithful wife of *ODYSSEUS*, the ruler of Ithaca, she was celebrated for her patience in waiting almost twenty years for his return from Troy. Beset by suitors, Penelope kept them at bay for a long time by pretending to weave a shroud for her father-in-law Laertes. Each night she would secretly unravel the day's work. Eventually, the return of Odysseus saved her from an enforced second marriage, but she remained cold towards her saviour until she was absolutely certain of his identity. Penelope refused to be convinced that the new arrival really was Odysseus until he described their bed, carved in part from a tree trunk still rooted in the ground.

PERSEPHONE was the daughter of *ZEUS* and *DEMETER*, the earth goddess, and became queen of the underworld as the abducted wife of *HADES*. According to the Greeks, Zeus promised his beautiful daughter to Hades without consulting her mother. When Hades rose from the underworld and took his bride by force, Demeter was beside herself with grief. The goddess wandered the earth searching for her daughter, two burning torches in her hands. As a result the land was no longer fertile. Plants wilted, animals

PENELOPE (right), patient wife of Odysseus, shared her husband's cleverness. During his long absence, she kept her many suitors at bay by refusing to marry until she had completed a shroud which she secretly unravelled each night, until the suitors discovered her ploy. (ILLUSTRATION FROM STORIES FROM HOMER, 1885.)

PERSEPHONE (far right), goddess of death, spent the winter in the underworld, rising each spring to live with her mother, the goddess of corn. She symbolizes the seed-corn that is buried, rises and falls again in a cycle of constant renewal – a theme central to the Eleusian mysteries. (PERSEPHONE, MARBLE, DETAIL, C. 490 BC.)

PERSEUS and Andromeda (above) peer gingerly at the face of Medusa, reflected in the water. Burne-Jones' Medusa recalls the tranquil air and death-like beauty of the Greek Medusas carved on amulets and charms, which remind us that she was once beautiful. (THE BALEFUL HEAD BY EDMUND BURNE-JONES, CANVAS, 1887.)

bore no offspring and death stalked mankind. In the end, Zeus was obliged to intervene and ruled that Persephone should spend time each year with both her husband and her mother. Persephone could never return entirely to the living world because she had eaten in Hades' realm: a very old idea that strictly divided the food of the dead from that of the living.

The story of Persephone's abduction, disappearance and return parallels the fertility myths of West Asia. She may well have been a pre-Greek goddess, a deity worshipped by earlier settlers of the country who was later incorporated into Greek religion. Her association with the dead may have a similar origin. The Athenians, who were originally a non-Greek speaking people, referred to the dead as "Demeter's people".

PERSEUS was the son of ZEUS and DANAE, daughter of Acrisius, king of Argos. Danae had been shut up in a bronze tower in order to thwart a prophecy that if she had a son he would kill Acrisius. But Zeus visited her as a golden shower and Perseus was born. A terrified Acrisius placed mother and son in a wooden chest and cast it on the sea. The protection of Zeus, however, was enough to bring them safely to the shores of the island of Seriphos, where Perseus grew up among fishermen.

On reaching manhood Perseus was sent by the local ruler, Polydectes, to fetch the head of the GORGON Medusa, a very dangerous task. Luckily for the hero the goddess ATHENA hated Medusa and instructed him how to proceed.

PHAEDRA, seen here with her sister Ariadne and husband Theseus, was the unfortunate daughter of King Minos and Queen Pasiphae of Crete. She fell in love with her stepson Hippolytus which eventually proved to be her downfall.

(THESEUS WITH ARIADNE AND PHAEDRA BY BENEDETTO GENNARI THE YOUNGER, CANVAS, 1702.)

First he visited the Graiae, three old hags who shared a single eye. Perseus seized the eye and obliged the Graiae to tell him about the nature of the Gorgons, their three dreadful sisters.

Most important of all, they informed him how a direct glance from Medusa's eyes would turn him to stone. He also received three useful gifts from some friendly nymphs: a cap of invisibility, winged shoes and a bag for Medusa's head. Ready for the exploit at last, Perseus put on the shoes and flew to the Gorgon's cave in the far west. Careful not to look at Medusa directly, he approached by watching her reflection in his shield. Having cut off Medusa's head and stowed it in his bag, Perseus flew away unseen by her two sisters.

The chilling powers of the head were used to good purpose by Perseus on his way home. Having

saved the beautiful ANDROMEDA from a sea monster, he married her, but several people had to be turned to stone before he and his bride returned safely to Danae. Having returned his magical equipment to HERMES, the messenger god, Perseus visited Argos only to find that Acrisius had already fled to Larissa on hearing of his grandson's arrival. The prophecy was fulfilled, nevertheless, when Perseus was invited to compete in the games at Larissa and his discus hit the old man on the head.

Because of the accident the hero chose to be king of Tiryns rather than Argos. On hearing of their deaths Athena placed both Perseus and Andromeda in the sky as constellations. (See also HEROES)

PHAEDRA was the daughter of King MINOS and Queen PASIPHAE of Crete. According to the Greeks, the Athenian hero THESEUS made

her his second wife. He seems to have abandoned her sister ARIADNE not long after she helped him kill the MINOTAUR, the bull-headed creature kept in the Labyrinth at Knossos. Like her mother Pasiphae, who gave birth to the Minotaur, Phaedra was soon overcome by an illicit desire. It was not for an animal this time, but for her stepson, Hippolytus, the son of Theseus' earlier marriage to the queen of the AMAZONS, Hippolyta. When she saw how Hippolytus was horrified by her passion for him, Phaedra hanged herself and left a message to Theseus saying that his son had tried to rape her. Theseus exiled his son, who was later killed in a chariot accident. In another version, Theseus cursed his son and asked POSEIDON to destroy Hippolytus, which he did by sending a seamonster. Phaedra, filled with sorrow, then killed herself.

PHAETHON was the son of the sun god HELIOS and Clymene, daughter of OCEANOS. He drove his father's four-horse chariot so fast that he lost control and threatened the world with a terrible heat. ZEUS stopped him with a thunderbolt, which sent Phaethon crashing to the earth. The great god may have also flooded the earth in an attempt to reduce the temperature. It was believed that Phaethon's mad exploit could be traced in the shape of the Milky Way, while he was reflected in the constellation of Auriga, the charioteer.

THE PLEIADES were the seven daughters of the Titan ATLAS, and were named Maia, Electra, Taygete, Celeno, Merope, Asterope and Alcyone. They may have become stars, or doves, in order to escape from the passionate intentions of Orion, the giant hunter. Their appearance in the night sky in May coincides with the beginning of summer, and the constellation of Orion then appears to be in perpetual pursuit of them.

POLYPHEMUS, a one-eyed giant, was in love with the nymph Galatea, but she scorned him, loving instead the handsome Acis. In a jealous rage, the giant crushed Acis with a rock; but Galatea turned her beloved into a Sicilian river bearing his name. (POLYPHEMUS AND THE NYMPH GALATEA BY ANNIBALE CARRACCI, FRESCO, C. 1595.)

POLYPHEMUS was the son of *POSEIDON* and the sea nymph Thoosa. He was a Cyclops, a one-eyed giant, and was thought to have lived on the island of Sicily. *ODYSSEUS*, during his long journey home, came to the island and asked for hospitality, but called himself Nobody. Polyphemus indeed proved to be a dangerous host and treated the Greeks as part of his flock, shutting them up in his cave and eating them one by one for his evening meal. Odysseus dared not kill the Cyclops during the night because his men lacked the strength to move the boulder blocking the entrance to the cave. So Odysseus thought of a cunning plan to enable their escape. He got Polyphemus drunk on wine and then put out his single eye with a stake. The injured giant roared with pain, but in response to the other Cyclopes' questions he cried out that he was being attacked by Nobody, so they went away, considering him drunk or mad. In the morning Polyphemus opened the entrance to the cave to let out his flock and felt the back of each animal as it passed to ensure no men escaped. But Odysseus and his men tied themselves to the undersides of the sheep and managed to leave undetected. For this crime against his son, Poseidon promised revenge on Odysseus.

POSEIDON was the son of *CRONOS* and *RHEA*. He was the Greek god of the sea, and the equivalent of the Roman *NEPTUNE*. He was particularly associated with horses and bulls. After the overthrow of Cronos, his three sons divided the world between them:

POSEIDON, god of the oceans, rode the waves in a chariot drawn by golden seahorses. With his three-pronged trident, symbol of his power, he shattered the rocks, called forth storms and shook the earth. (NEPTUNE AND HIS HORSES BY E K BIRCE, CANVAS, C. 1880.)

ZEUS took the sky, *HADES* the underworld and Poseidon the sea, while the land was ruled by all three. It was agreed that Zeus was the senior deity, though Poseidon frequently asserted his independence. Once he even chained up Zeus, with the aid of *HERA*, Zeus' wife, and his daughter *ATHENA*. Possibly because his element was the tempestuous sea, Poseidon was thought of as an unruly god. Earthquakes were attributed to his anger, and Hades was often afraid that the roof of the underworld would cave in because of the shaking Poseidon gave the earth.

Poseidon was pictured riding the deep in a chariot pulled by golden seahorses. In his hands was a mighty trident, a weapon capable of stirring the waters to fury, like the sudden violence of an Aegean storm. His wife was Amphitrite, a sea nymph whose name recalls that of the sea monster Triton. This fearful pre-Greek creature was turned by the Greeks into the merman. One of Poseidon's children by Amphitrite bore this name. However, the sea god had many other offspring by other partners. He even mated with the *GORGON* Medusa, much to the annoyance of the goddess Athena. From the severed head of Medusa sprang the winged horse *PEGASUS*, surely a favourite of Poseidon. Worship of the sea god was widespread among

PRIAM, the king of Troy, savours a moment of rare peace with Helen on the city walls, as she describes the kings and chieftains of the Greek host, who circle the city on the plains below. (ILLUSTRATION FROM STORIES OF GREECE AND ROME, 1930.)

the Greeks, although the maritime state of Athens did not always enjoy the best relations with him.

Because the Athenians chose Athena as the deity of their city, Poseidon flooded the countryside until Zeus brought about an understanding. The temple of Athena stood on the acropolis in Athens and Poseidon's own sanctuary was conspicuously sited on Cape Sunium, which majestically juts out into the Aegean Sea.

Another naval power that offended Poseidon was Crete. When its ruler, King *MINOS*, asked

PSYCHE *was so beautiful that Aphrodite became jealous and sent her son, Eros, to inspire Psyche with a passion for an ugly man, but he was so entranced when he saw her that he dropped an arrow on his foot, and so fell in love with her himself.* (CUPID AND PSYCHE BY FRANCOIS GERARD, CANVAS, 1798.)

the sea god for a sign, a white bull emerged from the waves. Religious custom required Minos to sacrifice the animal, but he chose not to do so, with the result that his own wife *PASIPHAE* became the bull's lover. Their strange union produced the *MINOTAUR*, the bull-headed man slain by Athenian hero *THESEUS*. (See also *FORCES OF NATURE*)

PRIAM was the son of Laomedon and the nymph Strymo, daughter of the River Scamander. By the time of the Trojan War Priam, the king of Troy, was already an old man, father of fifty sons, some by his queen Hecuba, the rest by other women. Although he disapproved of the conflict with the Greeks and its cause, Priam was always kind to *HELEN* throughout the long siege. She had eloped to Troy with his son *PARIS*. Priam was killed in the courtyard of his palace when the Greeks sacked Troy.

PROMETHEUS was a son of the *TITAN* Iapetus and one of the older Greek gods who sided with *ZEUS* in his fight against his father *CRONOS*. His fame was due to his affection for mankind, to whom he gave fire. Zeus, the leader of the new and stronger gods, had hidden fire away, but Prometheus stole it and brought it to earth with him. But this drew Prometheus into conflict with Zeus, who chained the rebellious Titan to a rock and sent an eagle to eat his liver. As this organ was immortal, it grew at night as fast as the bird could consume it by day. Prometheus was only released when he gave Zeus the information that the sea nymph *THETIS*, whom both Zeus and *POSEIDON* were pursuing, would give birth to a son

mightier than his father. By making sure that Thetis married a mortal ruler, the newly victorious gods protected themselves because her son turned out to be the warrior *ACHILLES*, an invincible but not immortal fighter.

Zeus' anger with mankind was on occasion explained by poor sacrifices. But Prometheus himself was not a straightforward helper either. He gave fire, an essential of civilized

life, but other gifts were perhaps less helpful. Out of the flaming forge came weapons of war, plus all the miseries that follow the disruption of a simple way of life.

PSYCHE in Greek religious belief was the "soul", but in mythology she was represented as a princess so beautiful that people adored her instead of *APHRODITE*. To put an end to this sacrilege, Aphrodite

sent her son *EROS* to make Psyche fall in love with the ugliest creature he could find. But when Eros saw her he fell in love and forgot his mother's command. They became lovers, though Eros forbade Psyche ever to look upon him. When at last she did, he fled in fear of what Aphrodite would do to him now the secret was out. In the end, however, *ZEUS* agreed that the lovers could be united for eternity.

GIANTS

GIANTS SYMBOLIZE IMMENSE PRIMAL forces, neither good nor bad, but larger than life. While Greek giants could be "gentle" guardians, such as Talos, the gigantic bronze man who defended the island of Crete, others, such as Geryon, were predators, preying on unwary travellers. Equally, the Cyclopes were orginally creative beings, making armour and ornaments in the forge of Hephaistos, and building the massive city walls of Tiryns. Later on they were also portrayed as moody, rebellious shepherds who ignored divine laws and preyed on mortals. The gods themselves are gigantic, especially the older gods, reflecting their primal nature, such as the Titans, and the Giants, who were beings with mighty torsos and snake-like legs. The Titans overthrew their father Ouranos, replacing him with Cronos, who was in his turn dethroned by his son Zeus. Such a cosmic struggle between older primal gods and a younger generation is a common feature in world mythology.

ATLAS (right), the "bearer" or "endurer", bore the heavens on his shoulders, as punishment for having fought against Zeus with the o divine Titans. The myth probably arose from the impression that gr mountains bear the heavens. In another story, Atlas, because he ref Perseus shelter, was turned to a stony mountain, named after him. Here, the heavens are depicted as a celestial globe showing the constellations. (THE FARNESE ATLAS, MARBLE, C. AD 200.)

THE CYCLOPES
(left), fabulous race of one-eyed giants, were initially regarded as creative craftsmen who helped Hephaistos in his volcanic forge, crafting special armour, such as Hades' invisible helmet, Zeus' thunderbolt and Poseidon's trident. Yet they were also portrayed as lawless, man-eating shepherds. One such, Polyphemus, here looms over Odysseus and his comrades who have rashly strayed into his den. (ILLUSTRATION FROM STORIES FROM HOMER, 1885.)

ORION (above left), who was one of Poseidon's unruly sons, was a gigantic and handsome hunter, who could walk through the oceans with his feet on the seabed and his head above the waves. Like his giant brother, the one-eyed Polyphemus, Orion was blinded in a quarrel, but his eyes were healed by the radiance of the sun god Helios. There are many differing stories concerning his death, but according to one myth, the love that Eos, the goddess of the dawn, felt for Orion was such that it caused divine jealousy until Artemis was persuaded to shoot him with an arrow on behalf of the gods. He was then raised to the stars to form a constellation. (ILLUSTRATION BY NICK BEALE, 1995.)

CACUS (above), son of Hephaistos, and a goat-like giant, preyed on human beings who strayed by his cave near Rome. Cacus stole Geryon's red cattle from Heracles while he slept, and hid them in his cave. However, the cattle began to bellow and Heracles came and slayed Cacus, retrieving the cattle that he had originally stolen from Geryon. (HERACLES SLAYS THE GIANT CACUS BY GIAMBATTISTA LANGETTI, C. 1670.)

R

PYGMALION was a king of Cyprus. According to the Greeks, he commissioned an ivory statue of his ideal woman, since no real one measured up to his expectations. Not surprisingly, Pygmalion fell hopelessly in love with the statue, an even more unsatisfactory fate than he had previously suffered. Because of his obviously genuine disappointment, the love goddess *APHRODITE* brought the statue to life and made it love him. Some traditions tell how the couple had a daughter named Paphos, who gave her name to the town.

PYTHON see *MONSTERS AND FABULOUS BEASTS*

REMUS AND ROMULUS were the twin sons of *RHEA SILVIA* and *MARS*, and the two founders of Rome. Rhea Silvia had been the only child of King Numitor of Alba Longa. When Numitor's brother *AMULIUS* deposed him, he also forced Rhea Silvia to become a Vestal Virgin, thereby ensuring that there would be no other claimant to the throne. But the war god Mars raped her in his sacred grove, and Rhea Silvia gave birth to Romulus and Remus.

Amulius ordered his servants to kill the new-born twins, but instead they cast them on the Tiber. Their cradle was carried swiftly away and eventually came to rest on a mudbank. To look after his children Mars sent his sacred animal, the wolf. Later Romulus and Remus were discovered in the wolf's lair by a shepherd named Faustulus, who took the foundlings home. So they were raised as shepherds, although the ability of the brothers to lead others, and to fight, eventually became widely known. One day Numitor met Remus and guessed who he was and so the lost grandchildren were reunited with him, but they were not content to live quietly in Alba Longa. Instead, they went off and founded a city of their own – Rome. A quarrel, however,

REMUS AND ROMULUS (above) were set adrift on the Tiber by Amulius, but the cradle came ashore and was found by a shewolf. The twins (left) march triumphantly from Alba Longa. On the left, Romulus bears aloft the head of their treacherous uncle, Amulius. On the right, Remus carries the wild head of Camers, a priest who counselled the king to drown the twins. (ILLUSTRATIONS FROM LAYS OF ANCIENT ROME, 1881.)

RHEA SILVIA (below), a vestal virgin, was loved by Mars, and bore him twin sons, Romulus and Remus. For violating the laws of her holy order, she was thrown into the Tiber, but the god of the river, Tibernus, saved and married her. (MARS WITH RHEA SILVIA BY FRANCESCO DEL COSSA, FRESCO, 1476.)

SARPEDON is lifted by Thanatos (Death) and Hypnos (Sleep) from the battlefield of Troy. This Lycian ruler, an ally of the Trojans, was later confused with Zeus' son of the same name. (ILLUSTRATION FROM STORIES FROM HOMER, 1885.)

ensued and Romulus killed Remus, possibly with a blow from a spade. Though he showed remorse at the funeral, Romulus ruled Rome with a strong hand and the city flourished. It was a haven for runaway slaves and other fugitives, but suffered from a shortage of women, which Romulus overcame by arranging for the capture of Sabine women at a nearby festival. After a reign of forty years he disappeared to become, some of his subjects believed, the war god Quirinus.

The Romulus and Remus myth was as popular as that of *AENEAS*. From the beginning of republican times, around 507 BC, the she-wolf became the symbol of Roman nationhood. (See also *FOUNDERS*)

RHADAMANTHYS was the son of *EUROPA* and *ZEUS*, and the brother of *MINOS* and *SARPEDON*. According to one tradition he married *ALCMENE* after the death of her husband Amphitryon. Others say that he was one of the three Judges of the Dead and lived in the paradise of Elysium, in the far west.

RHEA was the daughter of Ouranos and *GAIA*. As the wife of *CRONOS*, she bore six children, the hearth goddess Hestia, the goddess of vegetation *DEMETER*, the earth goddess *HERA*, the underworld god *HADES*, the sea god *POSEIDON* and *ZEUS*, the sky god. Cronos, having learned that one of his children would depose him, swallowed all of them, except for Zeus, as they were born. Rhea substituted the baby Zeus with a stone wrapped in swaddling clothes. He was then taken to the island of Crete, where the worship of Rhea was notable, and was secretly raised.

RHEA SILVIA was the mother of *REMUS AND ROMULUS*. She was the only child of Numitor, the king of Alba Longa. When he was deposed by his younger brother *AMULIUS*, the new king forced Rhea Silvia to become a Vestal Virgin. However, Amulius could not guarantee Rhea Silvia's protection from the attentions of the gods and she was raped by *MARS* in his sacred grove. Her twin sons were then cast into the swollen Tiber, where she may have been drowned.

ROMULUS see *REMUS*

SARPEDON was the son of *ZEUS* and *EUROPA*. He was adopted by Asterius, king of Crete. Sarpedon quarrelled with one of his brothers, *MINOS*, over the throne of Crete and fled to Asia Minor, where he founded the Greek city of Miletus. It is said that Zeus allowed him to live to a great age.

SATURN was an ancient Italian corn god, the Roman equivalent of the Greek god *CRONOS*, though he had more in common with the goddess *DEMETER*. He was believed to have ruled the earth during a lost Golden Age. His festival, the Saturnalia, was celebrated in Rome over seven days and was held at the end of December.

THE SATYRS were the wild spirits of Greek and Roman woodlands. Their bestial nature was shown in their horse-like or goat-like appearance. They were mainly associated with *DIONYSUS*, the Greek god of vegetation, wine and ecstasy, and played a crucial role in his festivals. (See also *MONSTERS AND FABULOUS BEASTS*)

SATURN, *"the sower", was also regarded as an early king of Latium during a lost Golden Age. Here, with his daughter Juno, he is wearing exotic robes, reflecting the Roman belief that he was a foreigner who fled to Latium to escape Zeus. (JUNO AND SATURN BY PAOLO VERONESE, CANVAS 1553–55.)*

SCYLLA see *MONSTERS AND FABULOUS BEASTS*

SEMELE see *LOVERS OF ZEUS*

SIBYL, in Roman mythology, was the prophetess who dwelt near Cumae, in southern Italy. One tale explains how she became immortal but still grew old. She refused the favours of *APOLLO*, the god of prophecy, so he condemned her to an endless old age. She was already ancient when *AENEAS* consulted her about his visit to the underworld. Another story concerns the famous Sibylline Books, which were a collection of oracles that detailed Rome's destiny. These were offered for sale to Rome during the rule of the Etruscan kings.

SIBYL, the gifted seer, foretold the destiny of Rome as predicted in the Sibylline Books, which became a vital source of religious inspiration and guidance. (SIBYL AND THE RUINS OF ROME BY GIOVANNI PANNINI, CANVAS, 1750.)

SISYPHUS, the slyest and craftiest of men, was punished for his sins by being condemned forever to push a marble block up a hill only to see it roll down again. (ILLUSTRATION BY NICK BEALE, 1995.)

When the offer was refused, Sibyl burned three books and offered the other six at the same price, but the offer was still refused, so three more were burnt and then she offered the last three at the original price. In haste the Romans closed the deal before all the irreplaceable oracles were totally destroyed.

SILENUS was a jovial satyr, much given to sleep and drink. Bald but hairy, and as fat and round as his wine-bag, he was more often drunk than sober, but when drunk or asleep, he became an inspired and much sought-after prophet. (ILLUSTRATION FROM DICTIONARY OF CLASSICAL ANTIQUITIES, 1891.)

SILENUS was variously described as the son either of the Greek messenger god *HERMES*, or of *PAN*, the goat-like god of the pastures. He was usually portrayed as the elderly companion of *DIONYSUS*, the Greek god of vegetation, wine and ecstasy. In appearance Silenus was a fat, bald man with the tail and ears of a horse. Because of the kindness shown to Silenus by King *MIDAS* of Phrygia, Dionysus granted the king his famous and short-sighted wish for a golden touch.

SIRENS see *MONSTERS AND FABULOUS BEASTS*

SISYPHUS was the son of King Aelus of Thessaly and Enarete. He was known to the Greeks as the craftiest of men, and suffered for his trickery by endless labour in Tartarus, a place of punishment beneath the underworld. Sisyphus is credited with the foundation of Corinth. According to one tradition, he angered *ZEUS* by revealing that the god had abducted the daughter of a river god. Zeus therefore sent Thanatos, god of death, to take Sisyphus to the underworld. Somehow the ingenious king temporarily made Thanatos his own prisoner. When the gods again claimed him, Sisyphus tricked *HADES* into letting him return to earth. Having told his wife to do

nothing if he died, Sisyphus said that his body was unburied and the customary offerings to the dead had not been made. He must therefore see to the arrangements himself before he could be said to be truly dead. Finally, Zeus lost patience and condemned Sisyphus to Tartarus to pay for his lifelong impiety. For the rest of eternity he had to roll a block of stone to the top of a hill only to see it roll back again as it reached the crest.

THE SPHINX, according to Greek mythology, was the daughter of Echidna, either by *TYPHON* or by Orthus. A monster with the face and breasts of a woman, the body

of a lion and the wings of a bird, she was sent as a curse on the city of Thebes by the goddess *HERA*. The Sphinx guarded a pass to the city and asked all who wished to pass a riddle. Those who failed to give the correct answer were eaten. The riddle was: "What thing walks on four legs in the morning, on three in the evening, and is weakest when it walks on four?" The correct answer was Man, because he walks on four as a baby and leans on a stick in old age. When *OEDIPUS* gave the correct answer, the Sphinx hurled herself over a cliff and died. As a reward for destroying the monster, he was made king of Thebes and married

THE SPHINX, or throttler, perched on a rock at a pass to the city of Thebes and challenged all travellers with a riddle, devouring all who failed the test. In Moreau's chilling scene, the queenly, feline Sphinx paws her victims. (THE TRIUMPHANT SPHINX BY GUSTAVE MOREAU, WATERCOLOUR, 1888.)

the widowed queen Jocasta, and so fulfilled his tragic destiny because the queen was his mother.

The Greek Sphinx should not be confused with the Egyptian Sphinx. The Great Sphinx at Giza was the protector of the pyramids and scourge of the sun god Ra.

TARPEIA was a Roman heroine, the daughter of Spurius Tarpeius, the commander of the Capitoline fortress at Rome. She may have played a role in saving the city. A war between Romans and Sabines, a people of central Italy, had been provoked by *ROMULUS'* abduction of Sabine women to provide wives for Rome's men. One tradition says that Tarpeia let the Sabines into her father's fortress after making them promise to give her what they wore on their left arms, their shields. Another mentions only their bracelets. In the first version the Sabines realized that they had been tricked and threw their shields at her and killed her. The Romans could not agree how Tarpeia died but, whatever her motive was, real traitors were always thrown from the Tarpeian Rock.

TARPEIA, a Roman heroine, was crushed to death by the shields of the Sabines as they stormed through the gates of the Capitoline fortress. According to one legend, she had lured the Sabines inside, to trap them, so giving her life for Rome. (ILLUSTRATION FROM STORIES FROM LIVY, 1885.)

TARQUINIUS SUPERBUS

was the seventh and last Etruscan king of Rome, who reigned in the sixth century BC. His youngest son, Tarquinius Sextus, caused the end of the monarchy by raping the Roman matron *LUCRETIA*, which caused *BRUTUS* to lead a rebellion. Tarquinius was defeated and the Roman republic was established.

TARQUINIUS SEXTUS, as he fled the battlefield of Lake Regillus, was struck from behind. His inglorious death was recounted in Macaulay's lays: "And in the back false Sextus felt the Roman steel./ And wriggling in the dust he died, like a worm beneath the wheel." (ILLUSTRATION FROM LAYS OF ANCIENT ROME, 1881.)

THESEUS

was the son either of *POSEIDON* or *AEGEUS* the king of Athens. His mother was Aethra. The childless Aegeus consulted the Delphic Oracle and was told not to untie his wine skin until he returned home. He did not understand what the oracle meant and so visited his friend King Pittheus of Troezen. Realizing that Aegeus was going to beget a powerful son immediately after the celebration feast for his safe return to Athens, Pittheus made his guest drunk and put him to bed with his daughter Aethra, and so Theseus was conceived. Before he left for home, Aegeus took the pregnant Aethra to a great boulder underneath which he placed his sword and sandals. He told her that, should she have a son, she must wait until he was strong enough to raise the boulder before she sent him to his father's court. After Aegeus' departure the wily Pittheus said his daughter's lover was really Poseidon.

When Theseus came of age, Aethra explained that he was heir to the Athenian throne and he retrieved the sword and sandals. On his journey to Athens he slew several desperate bandits, a fearsome son of *HEPHAISTOS,* and a dreadful sow, the daughter of the monster *TYPHON*. At Eleusis, then a kingdom separate from Athens, Theseus was forced to accept the challenge of a wrestling match with its king, Cercyon. The aggressive ruler died as a result of the contest, so Theseus became king of Eleusis, which he later added to the Athenian kingdom.

On his arrival in Athens, Theseus learned that his father Aegeus was hardly able to hold on to the throne. Not only was the apparently heirless king challenged by the fifty sons of his half-brother Pallas, but, worse still, Aegeus had fallen under the spell of *MEDEA*, the former wife of *JASON* and a powerful witch. She hoped that her own son Medus would succeed Aegeus. Although Theseus hid his true identity, Medea knew who he was and persuaded Aegeus to let her poison the mighty stranger at a banquet. Theseus was saved when

TARQUINIUS SUPERBUS, a cruel and tyrannical king, sired a no less cruel and ignoble son, Tarquinius Sextus, who raped the Roman matron, Lucretia. She, in shame, killed herself. The outrage provoked an uprising and Tarquinius was overthrown. (THE RAPE OF LUCRETIA BY PALO IL GIOVANO, CANVAS, C. 1570.)

the king recognized his sword as the hero carved the meat. The plot was revealed, Medea fled from Athens with her son, and Aegeus named Theseus as his successor.

The next cycle of Theseus' exploits was designed to secure the safety of Athens. First, he dealt with Pallas' sons. Then he killed a wild bull that was ravaging Marathon, to the north-east of the city. He also overcame the *MINOTAUR*, the strange offspring of *PASIPHAE*, the wife of King *MINOS* of Crete. An annual tribute of young Athenians was fed to the Minotaur, which lived in the Labyrinth that had been designed by *DAEDALUS*. No one had ever managed to find their way through this maze, so when Theseus volunteered to confront

THESEUS' exploits are illustrated on an intricate Roman mosaic. At the centre of the Labyrinth Theseus battles with the Minotaur. On the left, Theseus and Ariadne pledge their love at the altar, while at the top, Theseus sets Ariadne ashore, deserting the unfortunate maiden on Dia, on the right. (THE EXPLOITS OF THESEUS, MOSAIC. C. AD 200.)

the Minotaur his father despaired. It was agreed that if Theseus should, by some miracle, survive, he was to change the sail of the tribute ship from black to white on the homeward voyage.

At Minos' palace in Knossos the goddess *APHRODITE* gave Theseus an invaluable ally in *ARIADNE*, a daughter of the Cretan king who fell in love with the hero. Princess Ariadne knew that the Labyrinth was so complex that the only way out was to follow back a thread fastened to the entrance. After Theseus had promised to marry her, Ariadne gave him a ball of thread and a sword. The hero entered the Labyrinth, slew the Minotaur and then set sail for Athens with Ariadne and the rest of the Athenian party. He then left the princess on the nearby island of Dia. It is thought that he was in love with another woman, but whatever the reason he was soon repaid for his heartlessness. As the ship approached Athens, Theseus forgot to change the sail to indicate to his father that he was alive. Aegeus saw a black sail and, thinking his son dead, threw himself off the Athenian acropolis.

The suicide meant that Theseus was now king of Athens, and he joined all the communities of Attica into one state. Apart from enlarging Athens' territory, Theseus also undertook a number of heroic exploits. On one expedition he captured Hippolyta, the queen of the *AMAZONS*, who bore him a son, Hippolytus, but she died shortly afterwards. Theseus gave the accursed *OEDIPUS* and his daughter *ANTIGONE* sanctuary at Colonus,

near Athens. But discord entered his own house when his second wife *PHAEDRA*, another daughter of Minos, came to desire her stepson Hippolytus, to the young man's horror. Although he promised to keep her passion a secret, Phaedra

was so humiliated by his rejection that she hanged herself and left Theseus a letter in which she accused Hippolytus of attempted rape. He was exiled and died in a chariot accident before his father discovered the truth. In another

version, Hippolytus was killed by a sea monster that was raised by Theseus' anger, and Phaedra, filled with remorse, killed herself.

Theseus later seized the twelve-year-old *HELEN*, daughter of *ZEUS*, as a future wife. He claimed that only she was worthy enough to be his wife, possibly because of her divine father. But she had powerful kinsmen, and her two brothers, the *DIOSCURI*, defeated the Athenians and drove Theseus abroad. He died on the island of Scyros, when its king, fearing the presence of such a man, pushed him over a cliff as he admired the view. It was believed that in the fifth century BC, the Athenian admiral Cimon went to Scyros and brought the hero's bones back to Athens, where they were kept in a shrine.

THESEUS AND SINIS circle each other in a battle of wits and wills. Sinis, the pine-bender, was a robber who killed by tying his victim between two bent pine trees and then letting them spring upright, thereby tearing the man apart. (THESEUS AND SINIS, RED-FIGURE, C. 490 BC.)

FOUNDERS

THE ANCIENTS BELIEVED that many of their fabulous cities were founded by the pioneering heroes and heroines of legend, such as Cadmus of Thebes and Dido of Carthage. In Classical mythology, the heroic ethic combined with the Greek ideal of *polis*, or city-state, to create a variety of dynamic founders who built such celebrated cities as Athens, Mycenae, Sparta and Thebes. The Greek *polis* was an autonomous, independent community of citizens, slaves and foreigners who gathered within and around a fortified city. Each city honoured its own hero who was also often its legendary founder, such as Perseus of Mycenae and Lacedaemon of Sparta. Mythic founders were innovative, godlike heroes, guided by destiny and deity to create a fresh, vibrant culture. Apart from leading a tribe to a bright new land, and building a strong citadel, founders often developed helpful new ways and customs: Cecrops of Athens, for instance, encouraged religious worship, while Cadmus of Thebes introduced an alphabet of 16 Phoenician letters. A city or tribe sometimes honoured its founder hero by sharing his name, such as Ilium, named after Ilus, the Trojans after Tros, and Rome after Romulus.

CECROPS (above), one of the mythic founders of Athens, and the first king of Attica, is depicted with a serpent's tail, recalling his origin as an aborigine of Attica. He divided the natives into twelve communities and founded the Acropolis, the stronghold of Athens, which was also named Cecropia after him. An innovator, Cecrops abolished blood sacrifice, encouraged the worship of Zeus and Athena and introduced basic laws of property, politics and marriage. (ILLUSTRATION FROM DICTIONARY OF CLASSICAL ANTIQUITIES, 1891.)

ATHENS (right), the splendid capital of Attica, owed its origin both to Cecrops, who founded the ancient Acropolis, and to Theseus who united Attica's twelve states into one, and made Athens their capital. The city divided into the upper town, or Acropolis, and the lower walled town, as well as three harbour towns. The Acropolis, seen here, rises on a steep rock, its summit once crowned with sparkling temples. Most famous of all was the Parthenon, built of Pentelic marble in pure Doric style and adorned within and without with gilded and painted sculpture. North of the Parthenon rose a great statute of the city's goddess, Athena, whose helmet and spear were seen from the sea. Athens, the artistic centre of the ancient world, reached its greatest splendour in the time of Pericles (460-429 BC). (THE ACROPOLIS BY CARL HAAG, CANVAS, C. 1890.)

ROME (above), the world-ruling capital of Italy, situated on the River Tiber, was founded in c. AD 753 by the mythic hero, Romulus. The Colosseum, seen here, was one of the greatest monuments of the ancient city, initiated by the Emperor Vespasian and inaugurated by his son, Titus, in 80 AD. The gigantic amphitheatre was designed to accommodate 87,000 spectators around circular tiers, overlooking a central arena. In front of the amphitheatre rises the triumphal Arch of Titus, erected in AD 81, to celebrate Titus' victorious campaign in Judaea. (VIEW OF THE COLOSSEUM BY LIPOT KERPEL, CANVAS, 1846.)

ROMULUS (above), the mythic founder of Rome, was suckled at birth by a she-wolf, with his twin brother, Remus. The twins had been cast into the River Tiber by their great-uncle Amulius who coveted the throne of Alba Longa, but their divine father, Mars, sent his sacred animal, the wolf, to save his sons. Later the twins were rescued by the good shepherd Faustulus who raised them as his own. Once grown, they left Alba Longa to found Rome, but the belligerent brothers bickered over the site and name of the future city, and Romulus slew Remus, setting the warlike tone of the future city. (ILLUSTRATION BY PAUL WOODROFFE, C.1920.)

DIDO (above), legendary founder of Carthage, supervises a team of architects and masons on the left bank of the bay. Dido had fled to Africa from Tyre in Phoenicia where her husband, Sychaeus, had been murdered by her brother, Pygmalion, who coveted the throne of Tyre. On the coast of North Africa, the local king, Iarbus, sold Dido as much land as she might contain in a bull's hide. By artfully cutting the hide into narrow strips, Dido managed to secure enough land to build a citadel, named Byrsa, or "hide". Around this fort, the fabulous city of Carthage flourished from 853 BC. On the right bank, the still, calm tomb of Sychaeus rises beside a new sapling, symbolizing the growth of Carthage. The girls and boys playing on the bank represent the future power and generations of Carthage; while the rising sun, likewise, symbolizes the rising power of the bright new city. (DIDO BUILDING CARTHAGE BY J W TURNER, CANVAS, 1815.)

TROY (above) or Ilium arose on the grassy plain of Troas by the foot of Mount Ida. Founded by the mythic hero, Ilus, son of Tros, the ancient city was named Ilium and Troja after both father and son. The famous walls of Troy were built by the gods, Poseidon and Apollo, in the reign of Ilus' son, Laomedon. The next king, Priam, ruled during the tragic Trojan War, provoked by Paris' abduction of Helen, wife of the Greek chieftain, Menelaus. At a critical stage in the ten-year siege, the Greeks dreamt up the Trojan Horse, a massive wooden model hiding within its hollow belly an army of Greeks. (THE TROJAN HORSE BY NICCOLO DELL' ABBATE, TEMPERA, C. 1560.)

V

THETIS was a sea nymph and the daughter of Nereus and Doris. She was the mother of ACHILLES, the great Greek hero. Because it was known that she was fated to bear a son mightier than his father, both ZEUS and POSEIDON gave up all thoughts of possessing Thetis, who was much admired on Mount Olympus, the home of the gods. Instead, Zeus ensured that she became the wife of a mortal king, Peleus of Phthia. Thetis bore him seven sons, but she was dissatisfied with the mortality of her children. She tested them with fire and boiling water, but none could withstand such treatment, not even the youngest boy Achilles until Thetis dipped him in the Styx, the river of the dead. Even then, she forgot to wet the heel she held him by, with the result that he was not totally immortal. About this time Thetis left Peleus and returned to the sea, although she continued to assist Achilles as far as she could during his eventful life.

TIRESIAS, in Greek mythology, was the son of a nymph, Chariclo, and Everes, descendant of one of CADMUS' own men. The blind seer of Thebes, he was so wise that even his ghost had kept its wits, and not been overcome by forgetfulness like the other inhabitants of the underworld. At the edge of the world Tiresias advised ODYSSEUS that he would never return home to Ithaca if he harmed the cattle of HELIOS, the sun god.

During his lifetime Tiresias played a part in several myths. For instance, he warned King Pentheus in vain about the identity of DIONYSUS, when that powerful god

THETIS, although an immortal sea nymph, loved her mortal son, Achilles, with all the care and tenderness of a human mother. She shared his sorrows, and rushed to his aid, ever conscious of his mortality. Here she brings him some splendid armour as he mourns Patroclus' death. (ILLUSTRATION FROM STORIES FROM HOMER, 1885.)

came in disguise to Thebes. As a result of Pentheus' refusal to listen to the seer, he gravely offended Dionysus and was torn to pieces by the god's frenzied worshippers, the maenads. Tiresias also confirmed the pronouncement of the Delphic Oracle that it was indeed King OEDIPUS who was personally responsible for the plague which troubled the Thebans.

The blindness of Tiresias was explained by two tales. One account states that the affliction was a punishment for seeing the goddess ATHENA bathing. The other story is a somewhat less traditional explanation. Tiresias one day saw snakes mating and struck them with a staff, whereupon he turned into a woman. After living as a woman for a period of time,

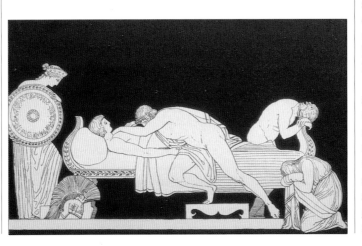

TIRESIAS, the legendary blind seer, advised many heroes. Some listened to him, but others, to their cost, ignored him, such as hard-headed Creon, or short-sighted Pentheus. His golden staff was a gift from Athena and enabled him to find his way like a sighted man. (ILLUSTRATION FROM DICTIONARY OF CLASSICAL ANTIQUITIES, 1891.)

the seer witnessed the same sight and became a man again. His unique experience led to Tiresias being asked by ZEUS and HERA, the chief Greek deities, to settle a dispute between them as to which sex got most pleasure out of love. When he said that it was the female, Hera blinded him, but Zeus awarded him a long life and the power of prophecy.

THE TITANS and Titanesses, according to Greek mythology, were the children of Ouranos, the sky, and GAIA, the earth. These gigantic beings were the older gods who ruled before the Olympian gods, who were the brothers, sisters and children of ZEUS. The Titans included CRONOS, RHEA, Coeus, Metis, Mnemosyne and Hyperion.

They came to power after Cronos emasculated his father Ouranos with a sickle provided by Gaia, his long-suffering mother. The eventual battle between the older generation of gods, the Titans led by Cronos, and the younger generation, the Olympians led by his son Zeus, lasted ten years and shook the universe like no other conflict. Afterwards Zeus threw those deities who had opposed him down to Tartarus, which was a land beneath the underworld.

The battle against the Titans should not be confused with the Olympian gods' later struggle with the GIANTS. In order to win this terrible confrontation, Zeus knew that he would require the help of a mighty, mortal champion, and so he fathered by ALCMENE the greatest of the Greek heroes HERACLES.

THE TITANS *were gigantic beings who ruled the earth before the Olympian gods. They overthrew their tyrannical father, Ouranus, and put Cronos in his place. Cronos, in his turn, swallowed all his children, except Zeus, who was raised in secrecy. Here, Rhea presents Cronos with a stone wrapped in swaddling clothes instead of the baby Zeus who is safely hidden away. (RHEA AND CRONOS, RELIEF, C. 400 BC.)*

supreme deity, but the recently victorious *ZEUS* destroyed him with a mighty thunderbolt. The volcanic activity of Mount Aetna in Sicily was believed to be caused by Typhon's imprisonment beneath the crater. The struggle between Typhon and Zeus was an evenly balanced fight, however. At one point Zeus was left helpless in a cave, weaponless and without his sinews. Fortunately the messenger god *HERMES* came to his aid on this occasion. Before his final defeat, Typhon sired the Chimaera, the huge sea monster killed by the hero *PERSEUS*.

VENUS was the Roman equivalent of *APHRODITE*, the Greek love goddess. Venus was originally a goddess connected with agriculture, but when she was identified with Aphrodite she took on a more active and different role in mythology. One of her most crucial actions was to return *AENEAS*' spear after it had stuck in a tree stump during his fight with the Italian champion Turnus. Indeed, in some versions Aeneas is her son.

TYPHON *(left), a fire-breathing serpent, was imprisoned beneath the crater when the volcano at Mount Aetna erupted. Symbolizing the dark forces of earth, he sired monsters as hideous as himself: the flaming Chimaera and snarling Cerberus. (GREEK VASE, C. 600 BC.)*

TYPHON was a terrible, serpentlike monster whose eyes shot out flames. He was conceived by *GAIA*, mother earth, when she was banished to Tartarus along with the other defeated *TITANS*.

According to the Greeks, Typhon endeavoured to establish himself as the ruler of the world, the

VENUS, *the Roman goddess of love, is rarely portrayed without her capricious and cherubic son, Cupid. This graceful portrait of her by the French artist Boucher, full of light and charm, owes much to Venus of Arles. (ILLUSTRATION FROM DICTIONARY OF CLASSICAL ANTIQUITIES, 1891.)*

X

VESTA was the Roman equivalent of the Greek goddess Hestia, who was the goddess of the hearth. Vesta, however, was worshipped both as the guardian of the domestic hearth and also as the personification of the ceremonial flame. Ceremonies in her honour were conducted by the Vestal Virgins, who were young girls from noble families who took vows of chastity for the thirty years during which they served her. Vesta's chief festival, the Vestalia, was held on 7 June.

VIRGINIA was the daughter of a Roman centurion named Virginius and, as with *LUCRETIA*, she was a Roman connected with a major constitutional change. Whereas Lucretia's rape and suicide led to

VIRGINIA (above) dies in the arms of her father who killed her to release her from bondage to the corrupt Appius Claudius. He then cursed the Claudian line, who were overthrown by the outraged Romans. (ILLUSTRATION FROM STORIES FROM LIVY, 1885.)

VULCAN (below), Roman god of fire, presents Venus with glorious arms for her son, Aeneas. The golden sword was described in the Aeneid as loaded with doom. (VENUS IN THE FORGE OF VULCAN BY FRANCOIS BOUCHER, CANVAS, 1757.)

the dethronement and exile of the Etruscan monarchy, the death of Virginia was a major factor in the ending of an aristocratic tyranny in 449 BC.

The lust of a corrupt official, Appius Claudius, for Virginia knew no bounds. He even dared to claim that the girl was his slave and used the law to have her handed over to him. At the last moment her father stabbed Virginia through the heart, declaring that her death was less painful to suffer than her dishonour. The Roman army rose to support him, along with the poorer citizens not then bearing arms, and checks were placed thereafter on magistrates' powers.

VULCAN was the Roman smith god and the equivalent of the Greek *HEPHAISTOS*. He was widely associated with Maia and *VESTA*, who were both goddesses of the hearth. His smithy was believed to be situated underneath Mount Aetna in Sicily. At the Vulcanalia festival, which was held on 23 August, fish and small animals were thrown into a fire.

XANTHUS was said to be the offspring of the *HARPY* Podarge and *ZEPHYRUS*, the west wind. He was one of two immortal horses belonging to the great Greek champion *ACHILLES* and had the power of human speech. Achilles inherited the horses from his father, King Peleus of Phthia, who had received them as a present from the gods on his wedding to the sea nymph *THETIS*. Achilles took Xanthus and Balius, the other wonderful steed, to Troy with him. They performed extremely well on the battlefield, although they seemed unnerved by the slaughter. When Achilles questioned them, Xanthus warned the champion that his own death was near, at which point the horse was struck dumb by the *FURIES*.

ZEPHYRUS see *FORCES OF NATURE*

ZEUS, *all-powerful father of the gods, enthroned on Olympus, is begged by Thetis to help her son, Achilles; she tugs his beard and clasps his knee in her affectionate way, as described in the* Iliad, *and the great god nods his assent.* (ZEUS AND THETIS BY JEAN-AUGUSTE INGRES, CANVAS, 1811.)

After the overthrow of Cronos, Zeus divided up the world between himself and his two brothers, *HADES* and *POSEIDON*. Zeus chose to rule the sky, Hades the underworld, and Poseidon the sea: the earth and Mount Olympus, which was the home of the gods, were regarded as common territory. A rare visitor to either of them was Hades, who preferred to be among the dead. Zeus' influence, however, was felt everywhere, although he had no control over destiny itself. Rather he was the god who saw that fate took its proper course.

The many lovers taken by Zeus, both mortal and immortal, form the very stuff of mythology. It is highly likely that they describe the coming together of several religious traditions, as Zeus incorporated the attributes of rival deities and gained credit for all important events. The continual antagonism between Zeus and his wife *HERA*, who was definitely an ancient, pre-Greek mother-goddess in origin, often broke out into major conflict. So jealous was Hera that she spent most of her time persecuting Zeus' lovers and their children. Once Zeus became so angry about Hera's cruelty to the hero *HERACLES*, his greatest son by a mortal woman, that he suspended the goddess from a pinnacle by her wrists and hung weights on her ankles. (See also *FORCES OF NATURE*)

ZEUS was the supreme deity in Greek mythology and the son of the Titans *CRONOS* and *RHEA*. The Romans identified Zeus with their *JUPITER*, an all-powerful sky god. The tyrannical Cronos insisted on swallowing all Zeus' older brothers and sisters as soon as they were born, but Zeus escaped this fate when his mother Rhea offered Cronos a stone wrapped up in swaddling clothes to swallow instead. In secrecy, Zeus was raised on the island of Crete. He grew to manhood determined to topple his father. The wise Metis, an early love and daughter of *OCEANOS*, gave Zeus the idea of a potion that would make his father vomit up all the children he had swallowed.

XANTHUS AND BALIUS, immortal horses and children of the west wind, "tore with the speed of wind". They were Achilles' battle steeds during the Trojan War, and wept for fallen heroes on the field. Here, Zeus leads them as a gift of the gods to Peleus on his wedding day. (ILLUSTRATION BY GLENN STEWARD, 1995.)

CLASSICAL FAMILY TREES

THE CHILDREN OF ZEUS

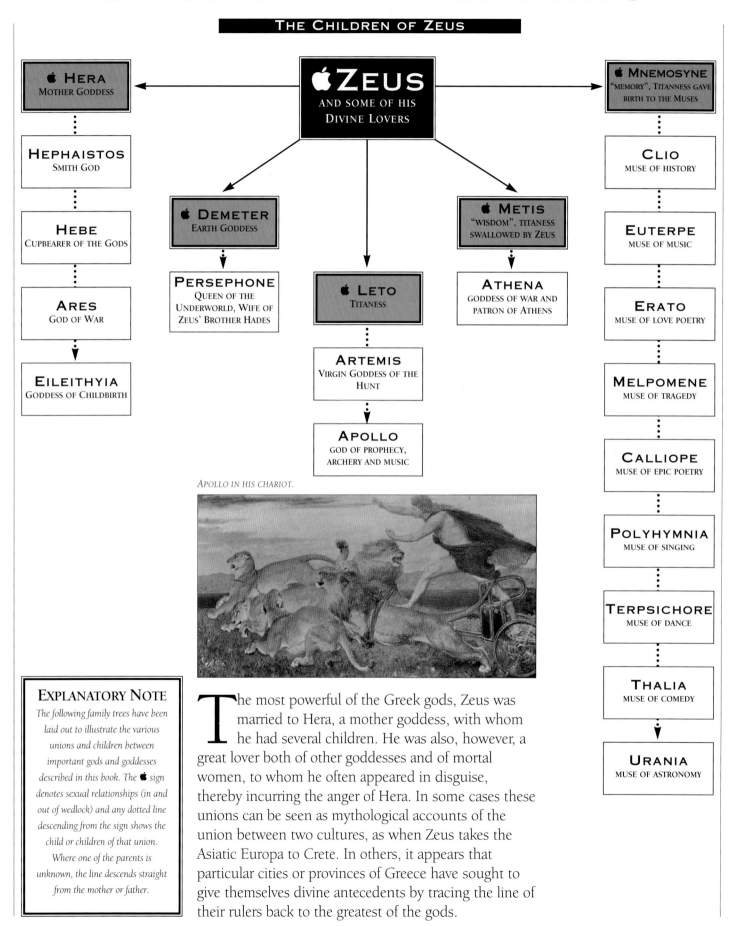

HERA
MOTHER GODDESS

ZEUS
AND SOME OF HIS
DIVINE LOVERS

MNEMOSYNE
"MEMORY", TITANESS GAVE
BIRTH TO THE MUSES

HEPHAISTOS
SMITH GOD

HEBE
CUPBEARER OF THE GODS

ARES
GOD OF WAR

EILEITHYIA
GODDESS OF CHILDBIRTH

DEMETER
EARTH GODDESS

PERSEPHONE
QUEEN OF THE
UNDERWORLD, WIFE OF
ZEUS' BROTHER HADES

LETO
TITANESS

ARTEMIS
VIRGIN GODDESS OF THE
HUNT

APOLLO
GOD OF PROPHECY,
ARCHERY AND MUSIC

METIS
"WISDOM", TITANESS
SWALLOWED BY ZEUS

ATHENA
GODDESS OF WAR AND
PATRON OF ATHENS

CLIO
MUSE OF HISTORY

EUTERPE
MUSE OF MUSIC

ERATO
MUSE OF LOVE POETRY

MELPOMENE
MUSE OF TRAGEDY

CALLIOPE
MUSE OF EPIC POETRY

POLYHYMNIA
MUSE OF SINGING

TERPSICHORE
MUSE OF DANCE

THALIA
MUSE OF COMEDY

URANIA
MUSE OF ASTRONOMY

APOLLO IN HIS CHARIOT.

EXPLANATORY NOTE

The following family trees have been laid out to illustrate the various unions and children between important gods and goddesses described in this book. The ● sign denotes sexual relationships (in and out of wedlock) and any dotted line descending from the sign shows the child or children of that union. Where one of the parents is unknown, the line descends straight from the mother or father.

The most powerful of the Greek gods, Zeus was married to Hera, a mother goddess, with whom he had several children. He was also, however, a great lover both of other goddesses and of mortal women, to whom he often appeared in disguise, thereby incurring the anger of Hera. In some cases these unions can be seen as mythological accounts of the union between two cultures, as when Zeus takes the Asiatic Europa to Crete. In others, it appears that particular cities or provinces of Greece have sought to give themselves divine antecedents by tracing the line of their rulers back to the greatest of the gods.

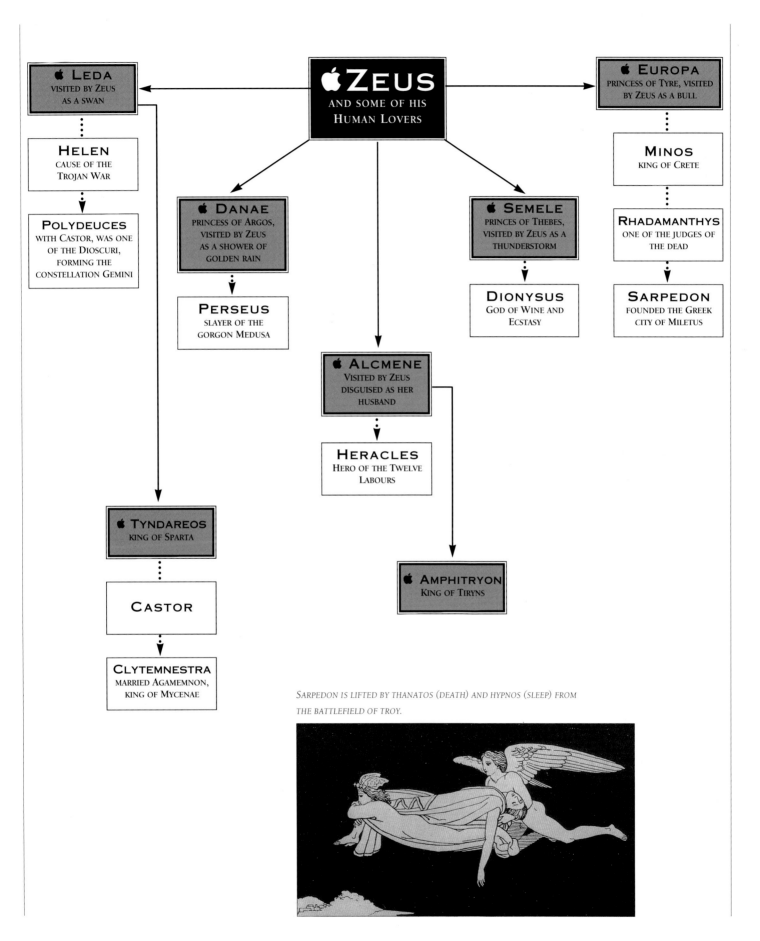

** LEDA**
VISITED BY ZEUS
AS A SWAN

HELEN
CAUSE OF THE
TROJAN WAR

POLYDEUCES
WITH CASTOR, WAS ONE
OF THE DIOSCURI,
FORMING THE
CONSTELLATION GEMINI

** ZEUS**
AND SOME OF HIS
HUMAN LOVERS

** EUROPA**
PRINCESS OF TYRE, VISITED
BY ZEUS AS A BULL

MINOS
KING OF CRETE

RHADAMANTHYS
ONE OF THE JUDGES OF
THE DEAD

SARPEDON
FOUNDED THE GREEK
CITY OF MILETUS

** DANAE**
PRINCESS OF ARGOS,
VISITED BY ZEUS
AS A SHOWER OF
GOLDEN RAIN

PERSEUS
SLAYER OF THE
GORGON MEDUSA

** SEMELE**
PRINCES OF THEBES,
VISITED BY ZEUS AS A
THUNDERSTORM

DIONYSUS
GOD OF WINE AND
ECSTASY

** ALCMENE**
VISITED BY ZEUS
DISGUISED AS HER
HUSBAND

HERACLES
HERO OF THE TWELVE
LABOURS

** TYNDAREOS**
KING OF SPARTA

CASTOR

CLYTEMNESTRA
MARRIED AGAMEMNON,
KING OF MYCENAE

** AMPHITRYON**
KING OF TIRYNS

*SARPEDON IS LIFTED BY THANATOS (DEATH) AND HYPNOS (SLEEP) FROM
THE BATTLEFIELD OF TROY.*

THE HOUSE OF ATREUS

TANTALUS
PUNISHED BY THE GODS FOR TRYING TO DECEIVE THEM

OENOMAUS
KING OF ELIS

 TYNDAREOS
KING OF SPARTA

 PELOPS
CHAMPION CHARIOTEER, GAVE HIS NAME TO THE PELOPONNESE

 HIPPODAMEIA
WON THE HAND OF PELOPS BY TRICKERY

 THYESTES
SEDUCED AEROPE

 AEGISTHUS
LOVER OF CLYTEMNESTRA

 LEDA

 ZEUS

 ATREUS
KILLED THYESTES' CHILDREN

 AEROPE
CHRYSIPPUS KILLED FOR THE GOLDEN RAM

CHRYSIPPUS
KILLED FOR THE GOLDEN RAM

 AGAMEMNON
KING OF MYCENAE

 CLYTEMNESTRA
MURDERED HER HUSBAND

 MENELAUS
KING OF SPARTA

 HELEN
RAN AWAY WITH PARIS

ELECTRA
RESCUED ORESTES FROM AEGISTHUS

ORESTES
KILLED HIS MOTHER, TRIED IN ATHENS

IPHIGENIA
OFFERED BY HER FATHER AS A HUMAN SACRIFICE

MENELAUS FIGHTS OVER THE FALLEN HERO, PATROCLUS.

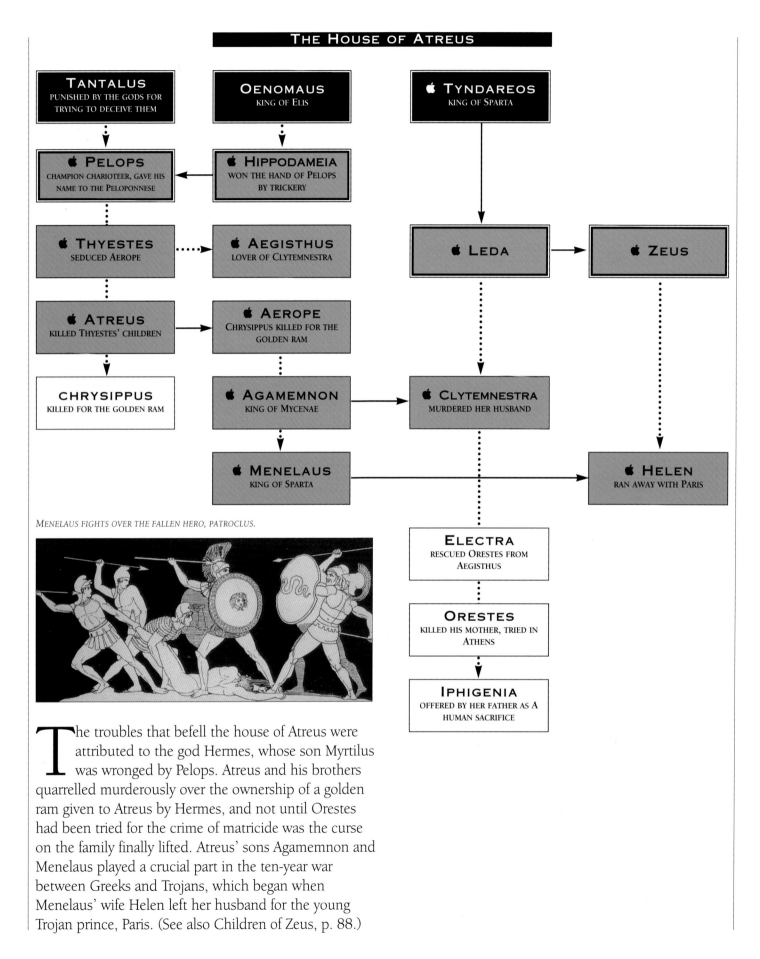

The troubles that befell the house of Atreus were attributed to the god Hermes, whose son Myrtilus was wronged by Pelops. Atreus and his brothers quarrelled murderously over the ownership of a golden ram given to Atreus by Hermes, and not until Orestes had been tried for the crime of matricide was the curse on the family finally lifted. Atreus' sons Agamemnon and Menelaus played a crucial part in the ten-year war between Greeks and Trojans, which began when Menelaus' wife Helen left her husband for the young Trojan prince, Paris. (See also Children of Zeus, p. 88.)

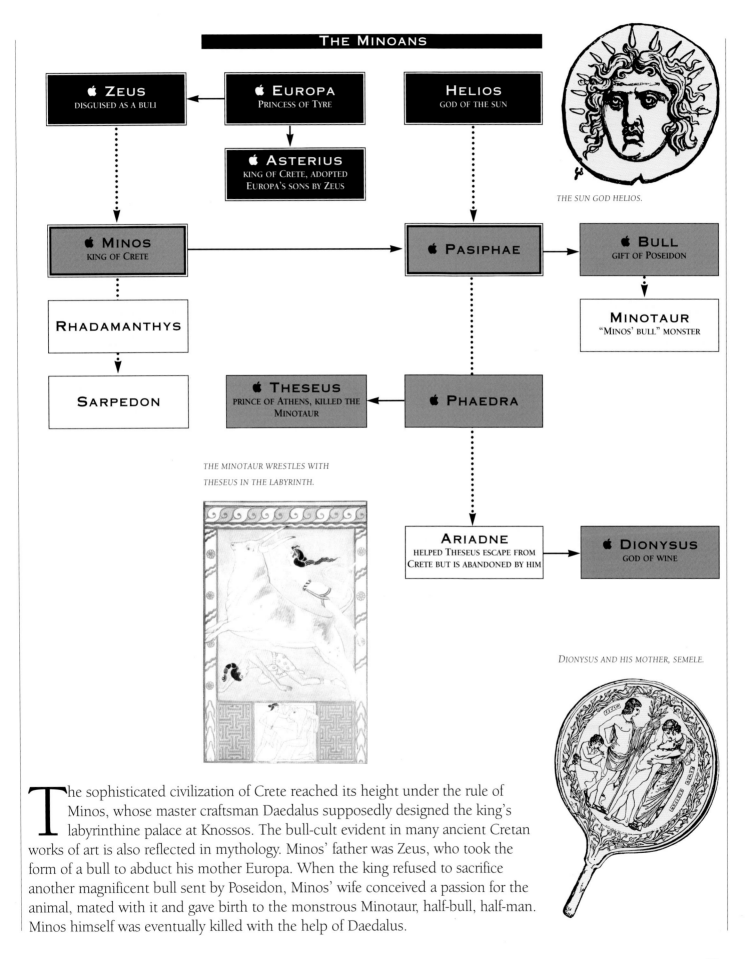

THE MINOANS

⬥ ZEUS
DISGUISED AS A BULL

⬥ EUROPA
PRINCESS OF TYRE

HELIOS
GOD OF THE SUN

⬥ ASTERIUS
KING OF CRETE, ADOPTED
EUROPA'S SONS BY ZEUS

⬥ MINOS
KING OF CRETE

⬥ PASIPHAE

⬥ BULL
GIFT OF POSEIDON

RHADAMANTHYS

MINOTAUR
"MINOS' BULL" MONSTER

SARPEDON

⬥ THESEUS
PRINCE OF ATHENS, KILLED THE
MINOTAUR

⬥ PHAEDRA

ARIADNE
HELPED THESEUS ESCAPE FROM
CRETE BUT IS ABANDONED BY HIM

⬥ DIONYSUS
GOD OF WINE

THE SUN GOD HELIOS.

*THE MINOTAUR WRESTLES WITH
THESEUS IN THE LABYRINTH.*

DIONYSUS AND HIS MOTHER, SEMELE.

The sophisticated civilization of Crete reached its height under the rule of Minos, whose master craftsman Daedalus supposedly designed the king's labyrinthine palace at Knossos. The bull-cult evident in many ancient Cretan works of art is also reflected in mythology. Minos' father was Zeus, who took the form of a bull to abduct his mother Europa. When the king refused to sacrifice another magnificent bull sent by Poseidon, Minos' wife conceived a passion for the animal, mated with it and gave birth to the monstrous Minotaur, half-bull, half-man. Minos himself was eventually killed with the help of Daedalus.

THE FAMILY OF THESEUS

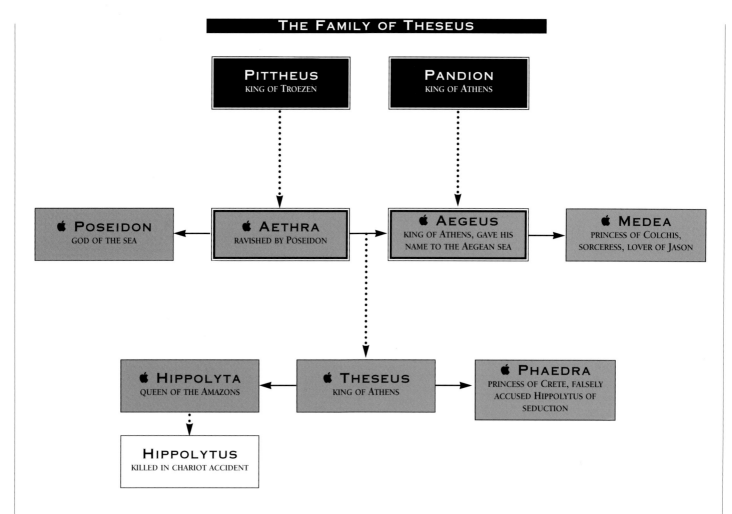

PITTHEUS
KING OF TROEZEN

PANDION
KING OF ATHENS

 POSEIDON
GOD OF THE SEA

 AETHRA
RAVISHED BY POSEIDON

 AEGEUS
KING OF ATHENS, GAVE HIS
NAME TO THE AEGEAN SEA

 MEDEA
PRINCESS OF COLCHIS,
SORCERESS, LOVER OF JASON

 HIPPOLYTA
QUEEN OF THE AMAZONS

 THESEUS
KING OF ATHENS

 PHAEDRA
PRINCESS OF CRETE, FALSELY
ACCUSED HIPPOLYTUS OF
SEDUCTION

HIPPOLYTUS
KILLED IN CHARIOT ACCIDENT

*THESEUS AND SINIS CIRCLE EACH OTHER IN
A BATTLE OF WITS AND WILLS.*

Although a mortal hero, Theseus was said by some to be the son of the god Poseidon. A brave fighter, he was a powerful monarch, uniting the twelve states of Attica into one kingdom with its capital at Athens. It was through Theseus that the two civilizations of island Crete and mainland Greece became closely connected, since he married the Cretan princess Phaedra, having abandoned her sister (see The Minoans, p. 91). Theseus himself died in exile, but his bones were eventually returned to Athens, where the people saw him as a saviour of the city.

THE HOUSE OF THEBES

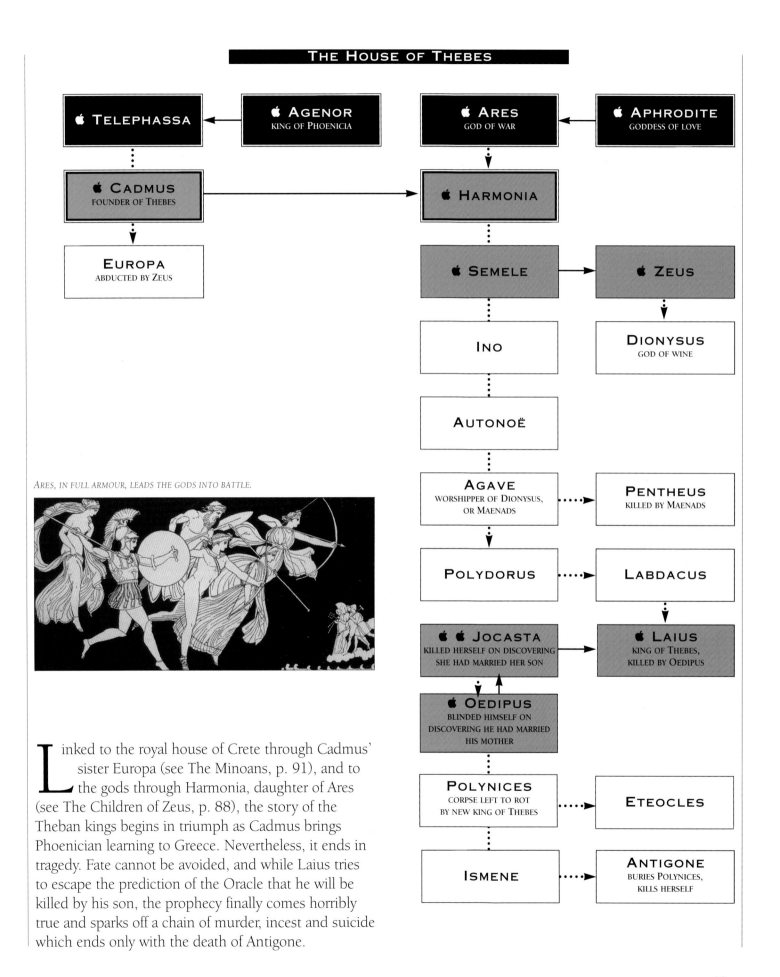

🍎 TELEPHASSA

🍎 AGENOR
KING OF PHOENICIA

🍎 ARES
GOD OF WAR

🍎 APHRODITE
GODDESS OF LOVE

🍎 CADMUS
FOUNDER OF THEBES

🍎 HARMONIA

EUROPA
ABDUCTED BY ZEUS

🍎 SEMELE

🍎 ZEUS

INO

DIONYSUS
GOD OF WINE

AUTONOË

ARES, IN FULL ARMOUR, LEADS THE GODS INTO BATTLE.

AGAVE
WORSHIPPER OF DIONYSUS,
OR MAENADS

PENTHEUS
KILLED BY MAENADS

POLYDORUS

LABDACUS

🍎🍎 JOCASTA
KILLED HERSELF ON DISCOVERING
SHE HAD MARRIED HER SON

🍎 LAIUS
KING OF THEBES,
KILLED BY OEDIPUS

🍎 OEDIPUS
BLINDED HIMSELF ON
DISCOVERING HE HAD MARRIED
HIS MOTHER

POLYNICES
CORPSE LEFT TO ROT
BY NEW KING OF THEBES

ETEOCLES

ISMENE

ANTIGONE
BURIES POLYNICES,
KILLS HERSELF

Linked to the royal house of Crete through Cadmus' sister Europa (see The Minoans, p. 91), and to the gods through Harmonia, daughter of Ares (see The Children of Zeus, p. 88), the story of the Theban kings begins in triumph as Cadmus brings Phoenician learning to Greece. Nevertheless, it ends in tragedy. Fate cannot be avoided, and while Laius tries to escape the prediction of the Oracle that he will be killed by his son, the prophecy finally comes horribly true and sparks off a chain of murder, incest and suicide which ends only with the death of Antigone.

INDEX

Page numbers in **bold** type refer to illustrations.

PICTURE ACKNOWLEDGEMENTS

The Publishers gratefully acknowledge the following for permission to reproduce the illustrations indicated.

Archiv fur Kunst und Geschichte: 1, 2, 10, 11BL, 12B, 13T, 14T, 16L, 17T, 18 (all), 19L, 21, 22, 28 (all), 32BR, 32TR, 33, 34L, 36TR, 37T, 38R, 39T, 39BR, 41R, 42TR, 43, 45T, 46TL, 47TL, 48BL, 50TR, 51 (both), 53 (both), 54T, 55T, 56BR, 57T, 57B, 58, 59TR, 60T, 61T, 62T, 63T, 64T, 64BR, 65T, 66B, 67BR, 68TR, 70T, 72TL, 73, 74, 76B, 77B, 78T, 79TM, 80T, 81 (both), 85T, 85BL, 86B, 87T.

The Bridgeman Art Library: 71: Bristol Museum and Art Gallery: 82B/Kunsthistorisches Museum, Vienna: 75BR/The National Gallery, London: 83BL/Galerie Estense, Modena: 83BR.

Board of Trustees of the National Museums and Galleries on Merseyside (Walker Art Gallery): 61B.

E. T. Archive: 29TR, 48TR, 49BR, 66T, 83TL.

Fine Art Photographic Library: 72BR.

Alan Lee: 42BR.

Manchester City Art Galleries: 15B, 50BL.

Scala, Florence: 27TL.

The Tate Gallery, London: 40T.